Dos and Don'ts of Completing the Ed.D. Dissertation

Dos and Don'ts of Completing the Ed.D. Dissertation

Jan P. Hammond
Paula E. Lester

ROWMAN & LITTLEFIELD
Lanham • Boulder • New York • London

Published by Rowman & Littlefield
An imprint of The Rowman & Littlefield Publishing Group, Inc.
4501 Forbes Boulevard, Suite 200, Lanham, Maryland 20706
www.rowman.com

6 Tinworth Street, London, SE11 5AL, United Kingdom

British Library Cataloguing in Publication Information Available

Library of Congress Cataloging-in-Publication Data

Names: Hammond, Jan P., 1948- author. | Lester, Paula E., author.
Title: Dos and donts of completing the Ed.D. dissertation / Jan P. Hammond, Paula E. Lester.
Description: Lanham : Rowman & Littlefield, [2022] | Includes bibliographical references and index. | Summary: "This book covers the basics from A-Z needed to complete the dissertation for the EdD degree"—Provided by publisher.
Identifiers: LCCN 2021022515 (print) | LCCN 2021022516 (ebook) | ISBN 9781475850109 (cloth) | ISBN 9781475850123 (epub)
Subjects: LCSH: Doctor of education degree—United States. | Dissertations, Academic—United States. | Education—Study and teaching (Graduate)—United States.
Classification: LCC LB1742 .H36 2022 (print) | LCC LB1742 (ebook) | DDC 378.2/420973—dc23
LC record available at https://lccn.loc.gov/2021022515
LC ebook record available at https://lccn.loc.gov/2021022516

We dedicate this book to all our students, past, present, and future.

Contents

Figures

Tables

Preface

So, you want to complete your doctorate. We know the pain you are experiencing. We've traveled the same path you are on. We have seen the tears of our students and their levels of frustration, making them ready to quit, regardless of how much money they spent so far, how much time they spent completing coursework, or how much family life they sacrificed. How many doctoral students have never completed their dissertation, and, at best, have only ABD (all but dissertation) status! This is heartbreaking for us when we hear these stories. This is why we were compelled to write this book for you. YOU are not going to be one of those. You are going to complete your journey, and we are going to be with you every step of the way.

We have tried to cover every aspect, from start to finish, related to the dissertation process. This book is meant to allay the fears that come with designing and implementing a research study. It is meant to avoid common pitfalls using the *Dos and Don'ts* format. It is also meant to help you write a dissertation that will make you proud of your achievement for years to come.

In addition, this book is written to help professors who are chairing a dissertation committee for the first time (which was all of us at one time) and need a little professional coaching to assist them in aligning to their university's requirements. The suggestions for students to seek guidance from their chairs are also meant to aid dissertation chairs in their responsibilities.

We wrote this book based upon reviewing the Ed.D. process of many colleges and universities in the United States that have an Ed.D. program. We found that even though each institution has some differences in timelines and procedures, overall, most schools follow similar paths on how to complete the Ed.D.

Sometimes we introduce a topic in an earlier section of the book and expand on it in a later part of the book. Based upon our own experiences as directors of doctoral programs as well as doctoral chairs, we often find that we have to tell our students the same information several times throughout the dissertation process; hence, you will find us helping you the same way.

We know that struggling through the dissertation process is overwhelming, to say the least. So, in writing this book, we tried to support the process using simplicity and a little humor. We had fun writing this work for you. We thank our current and former doctoral students who made us smile, while plowing through the doctoral process, and thank them for providing us the opportunity of seeing the challenges of the process through their eyes. We are grateful for their willingness to share their examples to help you along the way.

We hope you also find some laughs in reading our comments and will delight in the enjoyment of completing a dissertation. Keep your eye on the prize, and know that you are soon to be in the 1 percent of people who hold a doctorate. Congratulations!

Acknowledgments

Many people, including family and friends, have contributed to the success of this book. First, we want to thank our doctoral students who were the driving force by asking the same questions over and over when challenged by the thought of completing a dissertation. We especially want to thank those who allowed us to use excerpts from their dissertations as examples to make this book come alive.

We are appreciative of the feedback from experts in the field, including Kathryn Lusteg, Ph.D.; Raghavan Parthasarthy, Ph.D.; and Lloyd Yeager, Ed.D., who spent hours reviewing our manuscript. We also thank Connor Parthasarthy, a high school senior at Madison, Connecticut, for his illustrations.

The editorial and technical expertise from Rowman & Littlefield Publishing Group was invaluable. Hats off to those who helped us every step of the way. Special thanks go to Tom Koerner, editor, who immediately saw the value of this book. Thanks also go to Carlie Wall, managing editor, who gave excellent advice.

We also want to thank our universities that supported our endeavors. Jan wants to thank State University of New York at New Paltz and Paula is grateful to Long Island University, Post campus, for giving her a sabbatical, allowing her the needed time to complete this project.

Most of all, we want to thank faculty and chairs of dissertation committees over the years who pushed us to write this book due to their own frustrations. May our words of wisdom allay the fears that accompany dissertation writing, and provide answers to the myriad questions that students continue to ask.

Introduction

FORMAT OF THIS BOOK

Your journey begins with our table of contents. Review it first to determine where to start. Think of the table of contents as a detailed road map to help you quickly find each next step on your Ed.D. journey.

You will notice that the book is divided into three main parts. Each chapter within these parts is organized in a logical and predictable sequence, necessary to guide you as you embark on each juncture of the journey: your path to completion. There can be flexibility within the chapters (as per your university's guidelines), but not in the overall order of the chapters.

Part I, "Before You Start," helps to prepare you for the skills, knowledge, and dispositions needed to complete the dissertation process.

Part II, "The Dissertation Format," gives you the nuts and bolts—from beginning to end—needed to write a successful and defensible dissertation.

Part III, "And All the Other Stuff," prepares you for your proposal hearing, your dissertation defense, the follow-up paperwork, and your new role in our profession.

Along your journey, you will notice that key aspects will be introduced and then expanded upon or emphasized in a later section to help clarify important concepts. Although you may have prior knowledge of much that is written in this book, we have specifically detailed each step of the dissertation process so that you will have all necessary information in one place.

Hints, examples, textboxes, tables, and figures are included to better visualize what is needed. The *Dos and Don'ts* format provides suggestions to speed up the process, while also saving you from common pitfalls. Tools, such as a timeline template and chapter checklists, keep you organized throughout the process. To save you endless hours of researching, the detailed index at the end of this book will support your search for key terms. Also, you will find that we have identified online resources to help you move more quickly through the process. Enjoy your journey!

HOW TO USE THIS BOOK

Of course, we know that you are going to use this book by thumbing to the section that is most important to you. We have written this book as if we are guiding a class in completing the dissertation for an Ed.D. degree.

The three parts (I, II, III) help you to quickly turn to the area of importance for you. We have boldfaced and italicized certain vital aspects throughout the various chapters in each part. We have used bullets, boxed items, and hints for you to quickly grasp key information. You will find dissertation examples throughout the book, some from our former students and some from us, to grasp complex concepts. The table of contents, tables, figures, and index will guide your thinking.

Doctoral students should go directly to areas in this book they need to focus on next. Potential doctoral students may want to skim through the entire book to determine if the Ed.D. process is right for them. All students will appreciate the beginning, middle, and end sequence to completion.

This resource will also be helpful to doctoral faculty and chairs of dissertation committees to minimize the number of times the same information must be repeated to their students. Those who are chairs for the first time will appreciate the ease in locating what is needed to advise doctoral students through the dissertation process.

This book covers the basic requirements necessary to complete the dissertation for the Ed.D. degree. It is meant to supplement your doctoral courses and other resources, such as in-depth educational texts and software relating to research and statistics. The answers are now at your fingertips.

I

BEFORE YOU START

Part I guides you through the initial decisions you must make to complete the doctoral process. Key information and terminology will prepare you for the demands of research and writing at the doctoral level.

1

So, You Want to Earn a Doctorate!

Otherwise, said by your family and friends, "Are You Crazy!"

COMPLETING YOUR LIFELONG DREAM

Yes, completing the dissertation and receiving the doctoral degree is your dream. Yes, it is a dream to which many have responded with, "Sure, you are going to finish," and a smirk and grin on their face, assuming that completing the doctorate is a near impossible goal.

But you are determined. Nothing is going to stop you now. You are ready to take on this new opportunity of completing the dissertation. You can see the "Dr." in front of your name. Your journey is about to begin. Now, let's get going!

How Good Are You at Completing Jigsaw Puzzles?

One simple way of looking at the process of completing your dissertation is by comparing it to solving a jigsaw puzzle, without being able to see the puzzle while you are working. If you are a novice, you wouldn't begin with a 1,000-piece jigsaw puzzle. You would start with something smaller, such as a 250-piece puzzle. What does this mean?

First, **select the topic**. Just as you choose the jigsaw picture that works best for you, now you must select the topic that best complements your expertise and interests.

Second, **find a dedicated workspace**. Just as you would find a place to spread out all the puzzle pieces where you will do your work and where the puzzle won't be disturbed by anyone, now you must secure a dedicated workspace that has accessibility to filing, a computer, and good lighting, and is quiet enough that you can concentrate and not be distracted. Sometimes your workspace may be less than desirable. You do the best you can do. We had one student with an infant who had to choose the kitchen table. But she finished!

Third, **outline your plan of action**. Just as you usually start with doing the borders of a puzzle—the outside pieces—now it's time to outline a plan of action.

Fourth, **begin to write your chapters**. Just as you look for patterns within the pieces to complete the puzzle, now begin to write your chapters. Some students start with the Literature Review section, some with the Methodology, and many with the first chapter that introduces their study. You may find that certain puzzle pieces don't fit where you first put them—and have to be moved to another section. This will happen to you while completing your dissertation. Do not be afraid to write something in one chapter and then move it later. (Thank goodness for *cut and paste*!) You will find that certain areas may need to be redone or given greater attention (known as *write and re-write*).

As the puzzle starts filling in, there may be faculty (known as *your dissertation committee*) who look over your progress and suggest what puzzle pieces should be done next so that you can finish faster. You are now on your way to completion. You can do it!

How Do You Choose the Right Doctoral Program?

What doctoral program should you choose? The following questions may help you to decide:

- How far it is from home?
- How far it is from school/work?
- When do the classes meet?
- Do they meet on weekends/during the summer/nights?
- What competent babysitters are available and at the times needed?
- How much of the program is online?
- Is it video-conferencing: synchronous (same time), asynchronous, or blended?
- Is the program blended or only face to face?
- How much does it cost?
- Are scholarships available?
- Does the university offer any teaching assistantships or fellowships?
- Does the university offer financial aid? How much? Any assistance?
- Does the university have staff to help with finding outside loans?
- What is the program's reputation in the field being pursued?
- What is the university's graduation rate for its doctoral program?

- What and how much academic support is provided for doctoral students to complete their dissertation?
- How does the university's program support future employment?

The first question you should ask yourself is, "When I am finished, what do I want to do with this degree?" This will help you to fine-tune your decision on which program to accept. If you are just concerned with obtaining the title of "Doctor," then any college program will probably do.

But if you want to achieve a higher position in your career—your field—or to truly become a scholar, then you should look to see where others in your desired field have received their doctorates. Often there are key colleges whose alumni are in high positions (government, school districts, agencies) with links to future positions because of their university connections.

If you want to teach in a reputable college and eventually receive tenure, spend some time selecting the best college with the best reputation in your field. Remember, this is a terminal degree. There is no higher degree than the doctorate. So, spend the money; make the time; ignore the travel time; and apply to the best place possible for you with the best reputation.

Is It Okay to Apply to a Remote-Learning Doctoral Program?

Not so long ago, online doctoral programs were not given the same respect as those programs that were taught on campus in a classroom setting. Since the pandemic of 2020, many more colleges are offering doctoral programs that can be done remotely (off campus), partially or fully. You will need to do your research to determine if the program is reputable (accredited regionally as well as nationally). It's also important to discern if you have the discipline and technology skills to continue your studies without being in a face-to-face classroom setting.

Before Enrolling, What Questions Should You Ask?

After applying, you probably will be asked to attend an open house at the college (or remotely) for the doctoral program and may have the opportunity at that time to speak directly to the director of the program. In any case, these are some of the questions you may want to ask:

- "How many credits are being accepted from my transcript?"
- "May I have that in writing, please?" (*Words of wisdom:* Keep the doctoral handbook and any documents, including emails, that you were given by the college when you started until you receive your degree.)

- "What is the average length of time to complete the program?"
- "What is the time limit for completing the program?"
- "What is your rate of completion?/How many of your students graduate?"
- "What are the prerequisites for the program?"
- "Does your program follow a cohort model? If so, describe it."
- "How much of the program is remote?"
- "Is a dissertation required or are three peer-reviewed published articles accepted?"
- "When do I start thinking about my topic?"
- "How/When do I get a chair/advisor for my dissertation?"
  Hint: The dissertation is your ticket to completion of the program.
- "What kind of support does the university provide?" (editor/statistician/writing center/research librarians)
- "How many statistics courses do I have to take?"
- "After I complete the coursework, how much do I have to pay to maintain matriculation while completing the dissertation?"
- "Does the university have a placement office?"
- "Where are your graduates working now?"
- "How has this program advanced alumnis' careers?"
- "Will the university recommend/support me for future positions once I graduate?"
- "Does the university hire its alumni?"
- "Am I too old (too young) to begin a doctoral program?"

2

Dos and Don'ts of the Dissertation Process

WELCOME TO OUR CLASSROOM!

Years ago, two doctoral graduates were asked to return to the college to speak to a new doctoral cohort. Drs. Donna Berger (University of Albany, 2003) and Rita Weber McKee (University of Albany, 2005) came up with a way to allay the fears of the next beginning cohort by presenting their experiences using a PowerPoint presentation program (or similar) that summarized the phases of the doctoral process, based upon Jan's lectures as their professor.

What Are the Phases of the Dissertation Process?

Phase 1: Enthusiasm. You are excited! You got accepted to the doctoral program; you completed the required coursework; now, you are ready to begin your dissertation!

Figure 2.1. Enthusiasm. *Connor Parthasarthy, illustrator.*

Phase 2: Disillusionment. You start trying to put your ideas down on paper on an appropriate topic and find that it is much harder than you initially thought. What is the problem you want to study? What are your research questions? What are your hypotheses?

Figure 2.2. Disillusionment. *Connor Parthasarthy, illustrator.*

Phase 3: Panic. How do you go about finding a chair and a committee that will be your guides through the dissertation process? This is harder than trying to find a venture capitalist to support an innovation. What if you never find a committee that wants to support your topic or your ideas?

Figure 2.3. Panic. *Connor Parthasarthy, illustrator.*

Phase 4: Search for the Guilty. Okay. Why is this so problematic? Who is making the proposal stage so difficult? Who is in the way? Why is the IRB (Institutional Review Board) not approving my first submission (or second, or third!).

Figure 2.4. Search for the Guilty. ***Connor Parthasarthy, illustrator.***

Phase 5: Punishment of the Innocent. Your chair and your committee are not accepting your latest draft. Many changes and additions! Ugh! It must be your committee's fault—they won't let you move forward. You start wondering, should you find a new committee or remove the naysayer from the committee? Does this mean starting all over? You feel that there will never be an end to completing the dissertation.

Figure 2.5. Punishment of the Innocent. ***Connor Parthasarthy, illustrator.***

Phase 6: Finished! You got the "go-ahead" to defend your dissertation. You are standing in front of your committee in a room full of professors, doctoral students, and family and friends. Your committee asks you to leave the room while they discuss your dissertation defense. You wait outside with the others for a time that feels like eternity. Will they approve you? Will they tell you to make revisions? Will they tell you that your dissertation is not accepted, which means you will have to start from scratch? The door opens, and a professor asks, "Is there a new doctor standing out here? Ah, congratulations, Doctor!"

Figure 2.6. Finished! *Connor Parthasarthy, illustrator.*

How Do You Begin?

The hardest part is starting. You will find *every* excuse not to focus on your dissertation. Believe us, you will find it better to mow the lawn, hang drapes, vacuum, do the laundry, or do any other chore that you used to hate, rather than to begin to write your dissertation!

Writing is painful. There is no way around it. This is why others equally as bright do not have their doctorates. Thinking conceptually is not easy, yet it is required before you can put one word on paper. Writing a dissertation requires (a) high-level reading and thinking skills, (b) the ability to grasp large ideas and to generalize, (c) the knowledge and adeptness of decision making, and (d) tremendous self-discipline.

You may have to tell your family that you are not going to the movies with them or going out for a burger. Rather, you will go to your workspace and—at least—try to add another sentence or find another article. Something is better than nothing.

Give yourself an allotted amount of time—maybe only 15 minutes is all you can do today. Don't get discouraged, because tomorrow you may become so interested in a particular area that you are working on and end up spending two hours on it, where time seems to melt away.

You need your own workspace. First, you must commit to finding a place that is conducive for you to complete hours upon hours of study. Your office/

workspace should have a designated computer, a filing cabinet of some sort, and a printer. Also needed is easy access to paper, pencils, highlighters, Post-its, file folders, paper clips, a stapler, scissors, and the like. Your space needs to be free from distraction, or at least the best that you can do, depending on your surrounding environment.

You need to control your time. No longer is it permissible for you to be tweeting for hours on your phone or binge-watching on Netflix, known as *vegging*. You must control your time; otherwise, it will be nearly impossible to finish this monumental task. Set aside a block of time every day that works for you that is realistic. Then you must adhere to it. Respect your time the same as if you had an appointment with your boss. YOU are your new boss!

You must have a plan. If you have ever planned a vacation for yourself, you know how to manage your time. You have an endgame in mind and now you must follow a critical path to complete it. You have an idea: you want to take a river cruise in Europe, and write a blog about it reflecting on the cultures—When? "Next July, one year from today." (In your dissertation, this would be the equivalent of your Chapter 1: Statement of the Problem.)

Next, you pick up travel books or peruse the Internet to determine which countries are best aligned to your interests and read, read, read. How did others explore this region? This takes quite a bit of your time—perhaps a few weeks or months—and finally you will feel that you have saturated your topic. You now know what is "out there" by learning what others have found (Chapter 2: Literature Review).

Then, select which method (cruise company and boat) you will use to ride the river. You want to have a smaller boat with less than a hundred people on board, rather than a larger boat. Be sure to select your cruise within a certain time frame so that you can book your ticket for the airfare to get to Europe. You book the ticket, you pack, you choose the key outfits that you need for the trip (Chapter 3: Methodology).

Now, the day has come to fly to Europe, and then you'll take your cruise. You have your notebook and you are beginning to record your trip. You organize it with highlights from museums in one area and restaurants and their cuisine in another. When you are done, you look back on your notes and media, and now you analyze your entire trip to showcase what parts are most meaningful (Chapter 4: Findings and Results).

Finally, you write a summary highlighting the adventures of your trip, what they mean, and the impact they could have on future trips. How can your experiences influence others who want to take a similar trip, but want to focus on a different time of year or different land excursions? What would you do differently if you took another river cruise one day (Chapter 5: Discussion and Conclusion)?

Looking backward, now fill in **a timeline** for yourself anticipating dates when actions for your dissertation are to be completed. For the doctoral process, this means that you must set specific goals for yourself that align with completing your dissertation, setting dates on your timeline for each goal.

This is how you complete your dissertation in a timely manner. Make sure to adhere to your university deadlines for awarding of degrees (e.g., September, January, and May), graduation day, and other areas that pertain to your receiving the degree (ordering cap and gown, invitation cards for family and friends, etc.). Also, make sure to include deadline dates for scholarships, fellowships, teaching assistantships, and financial aid. Be sure to ask the department secretary if there is anything else that needs to be added to your timeline.

Always keep a positive attitude. This is no time to let your ego take over. This means that when your chair/committee members or your professors tell you that your paper/dissertation drafts/PowerPoint presentations need to be improved by revising your work, you must have a positive attitude and just say, "Thank you. I will do my best." Put your ego aside and do not take their comments personally. Respect their expertise and recognize that their concern reflects your potential in achieving your ultimate goal.

Your professors know what it takes to earn a doctorate. They may suggest (a) changing the order of your study to make it read more logically, (b) expanding your review of the literature to better align thematically with your study, (c) using another method to acquire the necessary data to prove your research questions/hypotheses, (d) or simply that you should "start over again." *Do not freak out!* This is what we have all gone through. You will not be the first to be told that your work is not perfect. Relax. Make the changes immediately (within 24 hours if possible!) and move forward.

Hints: When you feel that you are overwhelmed in your personal/professional life, prepare yourself before meeting with professors because you may not be emotionally ready to receive constructive criticism. You do not want to become defensive just because you are on overload. Do not look at your professors as the enemy. They are your ticket to completion. "Don't shoot the messenger!"

You need to have stamina. Students have told us every possible excuse as to why they are on overload. We hear, "I'm swamped!" "I didn't have time!" "It's the busiest time of the year!" and on and on. The best of course is, "I'm pregnant." Yes, several have delivered their firstborn while completing their doctorate. So, unless you have this excuse, there aren't too many that beat it.

Our students have made it through hurricanes without power for weeks, deaths in the immediate family, hospitalization emergencies, weddings and divorces, changes in jobs with increased responsibilities, loss of income, and moving out of the country.

You must have discipline. You are in charge of your schedule. You and only you create your schedule. This is the time to set priorities. You cannot do everything. You do not have to attend every meeting, every holiday function, every family event, or do more work than is needed to complete a project. This is not the time to schedule a home improvement project; wait until you finish your doctorate.

Energy is not endless. If you push too much, your immunity suffers, your family suffers, and your work suffers. This is not a winning strategy. There are only 24 hours in a day, no matter who you are. Learn to pace yourself. Most of all, take time in each day to relax; have a cup of coffee; take a walk by yourself; or find a quiet place to smell the roses. Find a way each day to revitalize your inner core (and please don’t blame everyone else because you have no energy left!).

Benjamin Franklin, a scientist, invented the lightning rod, bifocals, the glass armonica, and the Franklin stove. As a politician and philosopher, he founded the University of Pennsylvania and Philadelphia’s first fire department; as a musician, he played the violin, guitar, and harp; as a writer, he ran a printing shop and was the postmaster; as a politician, he was ambassador of the United States and one of our most significant founding fathers. Rumor has it that when Franklin was asked, “How did you get so much done in a lifetime?” his response was, “I just do 10 percent more each day than the average person.”

What Is a Plan of Study?

As stated before, you must have a written plan to propel you forward in a straight line. It is a contract with the university. Within your first semester, you will probably be asked to sign a plan of study. Look at your doctoral handbook. A plan of study must be approved by your college before you begin your studies. Who is responsible to guide you with your plan of study? When does it have to be approved and submitted? Many universities assign an advisor to students. If this is the case for you, make sure to stay on top of it, in case your advisor forgets to contact you. You may be part of a cohort model, meaning your plan will already be set and you may just have to sign off. **Keep a copy** of your approved plan of study, as you may need to refer to it in the future.

The plan of study is your road map to get you from the beginning to the end of your doctoral journey and to ensure you are meeting the requirements of the program. Below is an example of an abbreviated plan of study (table 2.1).

Table 2.1. Plan of Study

Year One	Required Course (Title)	Course Number
	Required Course (Title)	Course Number
Year Two	Required Course (Title)	Course Number
	Concentration Course (Title)	Course Number
Year Three	Concentration Course (Title)	Course Number
	Dissertation Seminar	Course Number
	Dissertation Advisement	*Course Number*

How Timelines Make It Happen!

At some point in your program, you will probably be asked to create a timeline by your chair or advisor. Timelines need to include tentative dates, adhering to a *critical path method*, a project modeling technique that includes all tasks and their duration for on-time completion.

Have you ever wondered how some people seem to finish the doctoral process on a fast track? What were their strategies? Following a backward timeline may help:

- Think about when (the exact date) you want to graduate from the Ed.D. program.
- Now write that down at the end of your timeline.
- Next, write the starting date of your dissertation, which coincides with your first classes.
- Think seriously about your passion: What topic has driven you to enroll in a doctoral program?
- Once you decide, stay with that topic. *Don't change your topic!* Many dissertations with different foci can come from one topic. Stay with your topic throughout your coursework. That will make your journey quicker.
- Now do a backward design on completing your dissertation. Start with chapter 5 (Discussion and Conclusion) and work backward. Fill in every part of the dissertation process on your timeline. Remember, *a plan without a deadline is just a dream.*

Of course, the above fast track may not be realistic for you. Your chair or other professors may help you refine your topic, which may be too broad (or too narrow) to begin with. Be patient. Adjust your timeline accordingly.

Here is a suggested timeline for you (table 2.2). Fill in the dates as anticipated.

What If Highly Unexpected Events Destroy Your Timeline?

Yes, there will be several instances when your timeline gets pulled off track. Try not to panic or give up your dream of completing your doctorate. Financial issues, a new job with new demands, critical family matters, children themselves, and medical crises and pandemics can uproot the best-laid plans. When these concerns happen, just do the best you can. Maybe you have to give yourself an additional two years to complete your studies. Maybe you have to find another way to pay for the rest of your program. Talk to someone in your university about such things. They may have additional financial means or ways to help you through this last lap of your program. In any case, deal with what you have to deal with. You have made a significant investment (time, money, personal relationships). Don't feel guilty, and definitely don't give up.

GUESS WHAT: YOU ARE A SCIENTIST!

Perhaps you have not realized it until this moment: Welcome to the world of science! You are a scientist. You will be using scientific methods to demonstrate (a) your understanding of phenomena and their relation to the world in which we live, (b) your ability to use scientific tools to analyze your findings, and (c) your ability to convince your readers that you have carefully and methodically followed a rational procedure that accounts for outliers and perturbations that may have affected your findings.

What Does It Mean to Be a Researcher?

You need to have the background knowledge to explore your study's concepts and relationships. You need to follow a systematic plan to carry out your research. You need to not show any bias. You need to be able to take criticism. You need to be able to have others replicate your study by following your methodology. You need to be able to answer any and all questions regarding your findings. You need to have the patience to write and re-write until there is no more to be written. You need to report your findings so that others can use your findings as a stepping stone to new research.

Also, get rid of your mathematical fears. You will need to be able to understand statistics. It is not necessary to know the entire world of statistics, but you do need to fully understand the statistical measures that you use in your dissertation. You will also want to make sure that you understand the basic statistical tools, so that you will have a better understanding of the methods used by other researchers when you do your literature review. Most doctoral

Table 2.2. Sample Timeline to Complete Your Dissertation (Hammond & Lester, 2021)

Start Date	*Task*	*Additional Info to Accomplish Task*	*Date Completed*
	Apply and get acceptance to the college/university.	Make decision for best choice.	
	Apply for financial aid, scholarships, teaching assistantships, etc.	Include deadlines in your timeline.	
	Go the library! Learn everything you can about databases, interlibrary loaning, books, articles, dissertations, and anything else to get you excited about exploring a topic dear to you.	Introduce yourself to the research librarian. Review all the tutorials and instructional pamphlets. Explore the databases.	
	Within first courses, select a topic.	Choose a topic that is doable.	
	Complete IRB training.	Print out your certificate from IRB.	
	Research/pursue potential dissertation chair/advisor.	See if the college has a list of faculty with areas of expertise.	
	Complete additional university prerequisites, such as e-portfolio, and prepare for the comprehensive exams.	Review the doctoral handbook and check off responsibilities. Get notes and prepare for your comps.	
	Complete all required coursework (minus dissertation workshop seminars) to take Ed.D. comps/exams.	Review with chair when to take the comps.	
	Finalize dissertation committee.	Meet with chair and create committee.	
	Develop a realistic timeline to complete the dissertation for yourself.	Begin by meeting with committee members, and end with filing for graduation.	
	Settle on research questions and begin literature review (chapter 2).	Read peer-reviewed journal articles and respected/ seminal books that have impacted your topic.	
	Begin drafts of chapters 1 (Statement of the Problem) and 2 (Literature Review).	Work closely with your chair during this process. Number each draft with a date. Whatever your chair says to change, make corrections right away. Be sure to put in writing what was agreed upon and send it back to your chair as a record.	

Begin draft of chapter 3 (Methodology).	With chair, determine which method/methodology to use.
Schedule and prepare for proposal hearing.	Your chair needs to schedule your proposal hearing. Follow university guidelines. Submit in timely manner.
Submit completed application to IRB(s). If the institution where you want to conduct the study requires its own IRB approval, check to see how your university wants you to handle that.	If needed, make all necessary revisions and IMMEDIATELY return them to IRB. You CANNOT start study until IRB gives you written approval.
Once IRB approved, start implementation of study: recruiting, phone calls, interviews, recording data. Be cognizant of coding, body language, timing, and other hints that may help enrich your findings.	Follow your methodology's data collection, take copious notes (record), keep everything organized, keep all papers. Don't throw out until you receive the degree.
Analysis of the data: if available, use your university program(s); otherwise, be prepared to buy the appropriate software package.	Depending upon program that you will use, make sure that you have the appropriate computer software and hardware already installed and learned.
Apply for graduation; order cap and gown, etc.	Check university calendar/handbook.
Complete chapter 4: Findings and Results.	Send drafts to your chair. Revise asap.
Complete chapter 5: Discussion and Conclusion.	Send drafts to your chair. Revise asap.
Prepare for dissertation defense. Create PowerPoint presentation; make sure committee members have copy of full dissertation and slides.	Your chair needs to schedule your defense. Follow university guidelines. Submit revisions of dissertation in timely manner.
Make corrections throughout the dissertation; get final approval.	Follow university guidelines and send to ProQuest (and be prepared to write an article based upon your findings and send it to an academic journal).
CONGRATULATIONS, DR.!	Celebrate with family and friends.

programs make you take a few statistics courses to help allay your fears. So work hard at it and get an "A" in your statistics classes!

One more thought about statistics. Data can be manipulated (statistically) to convey deeper understanding of a problem. However, taking the average of data (summarizing the information) can be misleading, particularly when one looks more closely at the variances (measuring individual differences).

We know that this may not mean much to you now, but here is one example to think about. If you look at the population of the United States, one might state that the average American is European Caucasian. However, if you look at the variance, you will find a deeper understanding—that we are a multicultural society with over 350 different languages spoken, and the six ethnic categories sanctified by the U.S. government only scratch the surface of the number of different cultural groups there are in this country. For example, in the American Indian population alone, there are over 500 different groups (Norris, Vines, & Hoeffel, 2012). So, "average" only scratches the surface. Please be aware of that when you are developing your research questions, your instruments for gathering data, and how you are going to analyze your data. Also, try to better understand the use of descriptive statistics and inferential statistics.

What Is the Meaning of Research?

Research (continuous and dynamic) seeks to find explanations to an unexplained phenomenon. It starts with a problem and builds upon existing knowledge. The process begins by setting up a method of experimentation or observations, followed by data collection; then analytical decisions are made based on the evidence.

A dissertation means you have to do research. Okay, you definitely did not want to hear this. To begin being a researcher means that you must *read* the classic books on research. The two best books to read at this moment to better understand the meaning of research are these:

(a) *The Structure of Scientific Revolutions* (2012) written by **Thomas Kuhn** is a seminal book to read before you begin your dissertation. Kuhn (1922–1996) was a professor of the history of science and a social scientist by nature. He upheld that *normal science* was conducted in paradigms, expressed as agreements of theory, which are gradually extended through the process of solving *puzzles*. Kuhn felt that the central theory and the methodology of science are not questioned or challenged.

In his theory, Kuhn concludes that scientific knowledge is only as valid as the other forms of knowledge that supply the information for determining the paradigm. If the knowledge changes or is altered by new information, then the scientific knowledge changes as well. Kuhn referenced this as a *paradigm change* or a *paradigm shift*. Kuhn upheld that it is through these paradigm shifts that new scientific knowledge becomes apparent and, most often, it is at odds with current scientific belief and understanding. He believed that science is merely a series of puzzles to be solved with established information and content.

(b) *The Logic of Scientific Discovery* (1959) written by **Karl Popper** is also an important work for all doctoral students to read. Popper (1902–1994), a professor at the London School of Economics, was characterized as a natural or laboratory scientific philosopher. Popper felt that the best scientists posed strong theories; then they tested those theories; and then they disregarded the theories if they were proved false, known as *falsification*.

Popper upheld that science is made of theories that are testable that have not yet been proven false. He disregarded any scientific claim that did not come about through the process of the scientific method and that lacked supporting data and evidence. He stated, "Whenever we propose a solution to a problem, we ought to try as hard as we can to overthrow our solution, rather defend it" (Popper, 1959, p. 16). Popper did not support the traditional scientific method in the manner of conducting observations and then using inductive reasoning to identify patterns and conclusions based upon observations. Therefore, Popper upheld that falsification was the true methodology of establishing the scientific credibility of a theory.

In a Nutshell

Kuhn argues that the scientific method (cause and effect) is the key to guiding scientific research.

Popper emphasizes falsification, meaning that something should have the ability to be proven false in order for it to be used in scientific inquiry.

Keep these two books at your fingertips. If nothing else, they will look great on your office shelf. Kidding aside, the magic within these two books is that there is a subtle argument going on between the two researchers.

Additional books for reference. You may want to acquire a few additional texts on the research process to help develop your conceptual thinking. Listed below are a few texts that we suggest. Try to get the most recent edition if possible; however, used copies or online versions are just as good.

(a) Swanson, R. A., & Holton, E. F. (2009). *Research in organizations: Foundations of human resource development* (2nd ed.). Berrett-Koehler Publishers.
(b) Creswell, J. (2013). *Qualitative inquiry & research design* (3rd ed.). Sage Publications, Inc.

What Are Some Key Terms for You to Know as a Researcher?

Throughout this book we will offer vocabulary specific to our field that you will want to know when sitting with your dissertation chair or in a doctoral classroom.

What Is a Theory? As doctoral students, you may be asked to state the meaning of theory, perhaps during your comps (comprehensive exams), your proposal, or within class time. A theory is a statement of how reality works. One of the simplest ways of stating its meaning is, "Theory is a generalization—an assumption built upon axioms." A theory can be said to give a generalizable explanation of the relationship between two or more variables.

Theories look for patterns to help shape your research. They try to make sense of what one observes or experiences within a particular aspect of life. They can be taken from objective facts or subjective thoughts. For example, the theory of evolution is a social theory that explains human life. By the way, parsimony is always appreciated. It makes the theory much clearer to the reader.

What Is an Axiom? The term "axiom" is borrowed from logic. It is a concept that is assumed to be true, as per a starting point of a discussion or argument (e.g., The only constant is change.).

What Is a Law? A law is something that cannot be argued as it has been proven to the point of no dispute. An example is the law of gravity. Originally a theory, it has now been proven through countless rigorous studies and experiments to be a law.

What Research Designs Are Useful to Educators?

Action Research. Often used as a practical way to improve teachers' instruction, student learning, and the educational setting, action research uses data collection focusing on a specific problem and allows the practitioner to reflect on that issue.

Applied Research. Used as a way to improve an immediate problem or process, applied research (a) tests theoretical concepts to help in clarifying frameworks, (b) tests validity of theories, or (c) contributes to new understanding to further knowledge in a particular area.

Case Study. A person or a group of persons is examined to better understand the complexities you are studying, using both intensive and extensive review of the subject(s).

Descriptive Research. Descriptive research describes, records, analyzes, and interprets the existing environment/conditions through observation, interviews, or surveys. It can provide facts or evidence needed for further analysis.

Evaluation Study. Educators frequently utilize this means of research to assess or appraise an activity and how those involved performed. It is used to better understand the effectiveness of a social program.

Experimental Research. Cause-and-effect relationships drive this research. Manipulation, control, and randomization are used to secure rigor and prove (disprove) hypotheses. As it is sometimes necessary to compromise one of the above characteristics, a quasi-experimental study can be done.

Exploratory Research. Used as a means to explore relationships between two or more variables and categorical information, exploratory research is often used to determine themes that can be later used for more rigorous quantitative research.

Field Studies. These studies are used to discover key interactions within an organization or another natural environment to obtain data and knowledge for improvement.

Historical Research. This type of research can add great value to the field of education. It uses historical facts and secondary data to analyze information in a new way, using a scientific method of inquiry to get a clearer understanding of past events and to see their potential impact on the future.

WHAT DOES IT MEAN TO BE A WRITER?

Okay, your research is stellar and your hard work regarding content shines through. However, what detracts from your study is your inability to adhere to the standards of writing. This is no joke. Trust us. If you want your committee to read your paper, you must respect the rules of the game. This means you must use the appropriate professional format, using resources such as the Publication Manual of the American Psychological Association (APA 7th edition, which we will be using to guide you), the Chicago Manual of Style (CMOS), the Modern Language Association handbook (MLA), and A Manual for Writers of Research Papers, Theses, and Dissertations (Turabian-style format, similar to CMOS), or whatever your university prefers. Be aware that these manuals are periodically updated; you will want to finish your dissertation before the next edition is published, in order to minimize having to update your citations and other changes.

For the purpose of this book, we will adhere to APA (that may differ from the publisher's formatting style), which is geared for the social sciences and seems to be the most widely used format in our field, with over 15 million copies sold (Publication Manual of the American Psychological Association, August, 2019).

What Are the Dos and Don'ts of Writing Using APA Style?

***Do* purchase grammar texts.** If you struggle with writing, here are two classics that have helped us. Perhaps you still have them from your first year in undergraduate school. Reread your hard copy or download popular grammar texts, such as *The Elements of Style* (Strunk & White, 2018), which explains the principles of composition, the eight elementary rules of usage, and words most often misspelled; or *On Writing Well* (Zinsser, 2013), which explains the fundamentals of conducting interviews and addresses the common errors in structure, style, and diction. Time to dust them off.

(a) *The Elements of Style* by William Strunk Jr. & E. B. White. Though the first edition was written in 1918, there have been several editions since then. This book focuses on using clear, precise language. You can easily find used copies for less than five dollars.
(b) *On Writing Well: The Classic Guide to Writing Nonfiction* by William Zinsser. This is another book that has several editions. Zinsser's book focuses on the fundamental principles of writing well.

***Do* know the basics of capitalization.** Know what words need to be capitalized in **titles** (e.g., all words except articles and prepositions that are less than four letters). Within the **text**, you need to capitalize all proper names and trade names and their mnemonics (e.g., Fourth Amendment is capitalized because it is the name of an amendment; IBM is capitalized because it is a trade name). Also, pertinent to your dissertation, names of tests and measures are to be capitalized (e.g., Teacher Job Satisfaction Questionnaire).

***Do* know the levels of headings.** APA gives five possible levels of headings (see pp. 47–49 in 7th ed., 2020), which were significantly modified in the fall of 2019 for the new edition:

(a) First level (used as main topic): centered, **bold**, all words capped except articles/prepositions that are less than four letters;
(b) Second level (used as subtopic): flush left, **bold**, all words capped except articles/prepositions that are less than four letters;
(c) Third level (used as subtopic of second level): flush left, *italicize*, **bold**, all words capped except articles/prepositions that are less than four letters;

(d) Fourth level (used as subtopic of the third level): indent, **bold**, all words capped except articles/prepositions that are less than four letters, **insert period** and begin your text (not bolded);
(e) Fifth level (used as subtopic of the fourth level): indent, *italicize*, **bold**, all words capped except articles/prepositions that are less than four letters, **insert period** and begin your text (not bolded).

***Do* know how to format citations within the text.** Citations cause misery to most of our students. Pay attention to these rules regarding author/date:

Within text, you can cite just the author and put the year published in parentheses. Example: Maslow (1943) published his motivational theory.

You can also write the theory and then give him credit and the year in parentheses. Example: Hierarchy of needs is a key motivational theory (Maslow, 1943).

When using the citation in parentheses, use only the last name(s) of the author(s). Use a comma between the last name and the year. If there is more than one author, stay in the order as published and use the ampersand symbol (&), not the word, “and” as shown here: (Lester, Inman, & Bishop, 2014).

***Do* respect quotation rules.** Including direct quotations in your work requires that you know the rules. If the quotation is less than 40 words, you include it in your text, with quotation marks at the beginning and end of the quote. Following the quote, the author, year, and page number are enclosed in parentheses. A period goes outside the parentheses.

If the quotation is 40 words or more, it must be blocked (indent the whole quotation as if it were a paragraph—and ensure it is blocked). In a block quotation, you do not insert quotation marks. A period goes at the end of the quote. Last is the author, year, and page number inside parentheses (no period).

***Do* know how to build your reference list.** While citing a journal, book, and the like in your text, **immediately** place the full citation in your reference list. To get you started initially, you will need the following basic information (see reference list information in part II, chapter 9 of this book that includes examples and punctuations needed):

(a) Book: the author(s) name, the year of publication, the title of the book italicized (only first word and proper names capitalized), and the name of the publisher.
(b) Journal article: the author(s) name, the date of publication, the title of the article (only first word and proper names capitalized), the name of the journal italicized, the volume number, the issue number, and the page numbers. If retrieved online, then put in the doi/web address.

***Do* keep your reference list up to date.** In APA, refer to pages 66–67 and also chapters 9, 10, and 11 for more specific details on reference lists, reference examples, and legal references. Addressed in these chapters are how to cite tweets, Instagram posts, podcasts, Facebook posts and pages, Ted Talks, and webinars to keep you current with some of the new changes.

***Do* become familiar with statistical abbreviations and symbols.** You may not realize that there are accepted abbreviations and symbols for our field. APA has provided you with a comprehensive table (Table 6.5: *Statistical Abbreviations and Symbols*, see pp. 183–86 in APA 7th ed.) that highlights frequently used abbreviations as well as Greek symbols. We recommend that you take time to review this section, as you will need to have this knowledge when writing your dissertation chapter 3 (Methodology) and chapter 4 (Findings and Results).

***Don't* treat all numbers the same.** There are rules for how to write numbers. Usually, when the Arabic numeral is less than 10, write it out in word form (e.g., two, four, eight participants). If it is 10 or more, use the Arabic numeral (e.g., 10, 11, 21, 1006). If you are writing certain fractions within the text, for example, "two-thirds majority," it should be spelled out.

However, there are exceptions (see pp. 178–82 in APA 7th ed.). If numbers represent formulas (½ base × height), percentages (5 percent), ratios (5–4 judges' decision), then use the Arabic numeral. If any number begins a sentence, write out the full number (e.g., Two thousand twenty was the year of the pandemic).

Roman numerals (e.g., i, ii, iii, I, II, III, etc.) used in your introductory pages (e.g., acknowledgments, table of contents, list of tables) are to remain Roman numerals and not to be changed to Arabic numerals.

***Don't* be sloppy.** When professors read a paper that does not adhere to the publishing standards, it immediately shows a poor-quality paper and overshadows the brilliance of your content. We highly recommend that you read the APA manual cover to cover **even before** you begin your first doctoral class. You will find that everything is covered by the APA (attention to specifics, clarity in writing, paragraph length, etc.).

Make sure all words are spelled correctly and that you adhere to the rules of grammar. Use spellcheck, find/replace, dictionaries, a thesaurus, and grammar-checker software programs (e.g., Ginger, Grammarly, ProWriting-Aid, Scribens, and SpellCheckPlus, to mention a few).

Be aware that your spell-checker program may not know how to spell your field's jargon. Be aware of double words (e.g., the the) or the accurate spelling of words specific to your topic (e.g., generalizability), spelling of proper names (e.g., Karyn, Caryn, or Karen), specific medical terms, legal terms, or foreign words, and the like (see pp. 168–81 in APA 7th ed.). Words typed incorrectly by one or two letters (manure man vs. mature man) may also be missed by a spell-checker program. Be careful with autocorrect, which, by now, has frustrated you many times. Make sure you know the difference between *effect* and *affect*; *their*, *there*, *they're*; and *its* and *it's*.

Two Latin abbreviations that often confuse our students are *exempli gratia* with the abbreviation **e.g.** (for example), and the other is *id est*, which is abbreviated **i.e.** (that is . . . or, in other words). If using either one in your text, make sure to put a comma after it. For example, *Because of successful models of school choice (**e.g.,** Community of Peace Academy, Kipp Academy, and Roxbury Preparatory Charter School), Congress continues to support new legislation to fund charter schools (**i.e.,** publicly funded schools).*

Also, be aware of the bugs in software programs. One problem yet to be corrected in the auto-formatting of MS Word: spacing issues. In order to override spacing issues, go to "Paragraph," then "Line Spacing Options," then make sure all spacing options are at zero, including "special area."

***Don't* forget page numbers.** Page numbers are required; your title (cover) page is page 1; the introductory pages are Roman numbers; the abstract is numbered page 2; your dissertation's chapter 1 starts on page 3, and the numbers are continuous from there throughout the dissertation.

***Don't* plagiarize.** Plagiarism can get you expelled from your university and you can be personally sued. This is nothing to fool around with. Be aware that even if you changed a few words, you are still plagiarizing. Know the differences between plagiarism and paraphrasing. Paraphrasing must be cited correctly. If you are quoting parts of a written work, know the copyright laws of 1978, which allow you to use only a small portion of the work. Otherwise, you will need written permission from the author or the publisher.

Finally, *don't* insult or confront your professor. This is one time that you need to be humble. Every professor has something for you to learn. These words of wisdom echo the sage philosophy: "Never burn a bridge."

Remember, remotely signing on late or coming to class late is considered a personal affront, indicating that the class is not important. If you need to be late (or leave early), be respectful and **ask** your professor if you can be excused.

You must ask ahead of time for permission to submit an assignment past the date due. Otherwise, it is an unspoken blemish against your credibility (and such action may work against you if that is a professor you want as a committee member).

Hint: By the way, if you haven't realized it yet, professors talk with each other. Be professional at all times, which includes meeting deadlines, demonstrating your preparation for class by engaging in class discussions, and maintaining a positive attitude.

Why Is Your Study Important?

You are beginning a voyage of a lifetime! Your study will contribute to the body of literature that helps build upon the answers needed to better understand the concepts and theories behind human behavior.

VOYAGE OF A LIFETIME
No matter what faith you are, this dissertation is going to find you In Silence – many more hours than usual. It is during this time that you will start to think at a higher level— Not about the material world, but about a more spiritual world. You will find yourself seeking ways to improve the environment, relationships, And growth of individuals in your strife to reach a better place for all. YOUR THINKING WILL BE FOREVER CHANGED.

Figure 2.7. Voyage of a Lifetime. ***Jan Hammond and Paula Lester.***

This experience will change your thinking and make you a better reader, a better writer, and a better problem solver. It also will broaden your horizons, preparing you for a higher-quality career. Best of all, you will become a more tolerant, considerate, and open-minded person. However, we must tell you: the average weight that a person gains while completing the doctoral process is 10 lbs. So watch the number of M&Ms you eat during your writing sessions ☺.

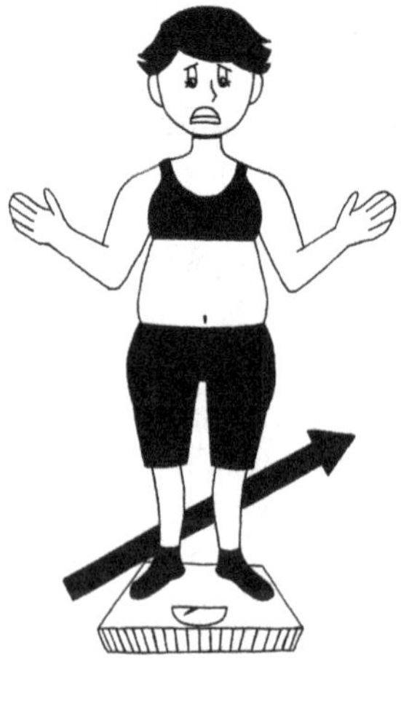

Figure 2.8. Scale. ***Connor Parthasarthy, illustrator.***

3

On Your Way to Becoming a Doctor!

OVERVIEW OF THE DISSERTATION PROCESS

Embarking on the dissertation process is much more challenging than one can imagine. It is nothing like completing your coursework, where you stay up all night to write a paper or complete an assignment, then have it graded by your professor. Of course, you will hear your professors all say that. But it truly *is nothing* like your coursework.

First, and as soon as possible, find a topic about which you are passionate. Start researching, writing, and studying it as you begin your first doctoral classes. What have others learned about the topic? What questions still remain? Developing your knowledge on this topic will help propel your doctoral process if you can write your first papers centered around it. Then, by the time you begin your first dissertation chapter, you should be well versed in your topic.

Second, writing and re-writing become the key to completing a dissertation. You will find it tedious and annoying, but your chair will continually tell you to re-write. It is part of the dissertation process. We can verify that almost every student at their dissertation defense reports that the hardest part was the constant re-writing: chopping, cutting and pasting, revamping, or throwing out sections that they thought were great but their committee did not. Perhaps this is where *fear* enters: the student who has not completed the process and is in the audience, viewing another student's defense. This is normal, because you may be at the struggling stage. No reason to fear. It's just hard work: perseverance wins. Writing a book, such as this, requires the same writing/re-writing process. The most important thing is to just jot down your thoughts before you forget them. Later, you can expand on them or move them to the appropriate section.

Third, respect the power of your dissertation committee. In completing the dissertation process, it is your job to convince your committee (who represent all those who have earned doctorates in your field) that you have mastered the knowledge, the higher-level thinking skills, and have the determination and the attributes needed to profess at the doctoral level. No matter how many "A" grades that you have to date, they do not solidify your claim for the doctoral degree. Only your committee (and perhaps the weight of some influential members in the audience who will try to sway your committee by asking pertinent questions regarding your methodology and findings at your defense) can bestow the acceptance (or not) of your dissertation as submitted (or as revised).

THE FIVE KEY DISSERTATION CHAPTERS

For those completing the doctorate in education degree (Ed.D.), there are five key chapters that outline the dissertation process (dissertation chapter titles are all caps):

CHAPTER 1 is the STATEMENT OF THE PROBLEM.
CHAPTER 2 is the REVIEW OF THE LITERATURE.
CHAPTER 3 is the METHODOLOGY that you used.
CHAPTER 4 is the FINDINGS AND RESULTS of your study.
CHAPTER 5 is the DISCUSSION AND CONCLUSION of your study.

What Is the Difference Between Ph.D. and Ed.D.?

One of the first questions that prospective students ask is, "What is the difference between Ed.D. and Ph.D.?" Confirm that the program you select has the degree that you want. The following should help you better understand the difference.

Ph.D. The objective of the Ph.D. (doctor of philosophy) is a philosophical degree. The purpose for one who chooses this degree is to broaden academic knowledge by creating or expanding a theoretical model, advancing experimental **original** research, and defending rigorous data analysis. Students completing the Ph.D. are often required to have an additional theoretical **chapter**, developing and/or embellishing a theoretical model. Model building precedes the methodology section. Ph.D. students usually take an additional course in constructing models.

Ed.D. The objective of the Ed.D. (doctor in education), which is the basis of this book, is a practitioner's degree that focuses on research for the benefit of improving educational systems. Those who earn the doctorate in education use their knowledge gained from the degree process in educational areas such as policy development at the state and federal levels; administration and leadership in schools; curriculum development; finance and budgeting; special education and pupil personnel; human resources; leading the pedagogy of fine arts, physical education, and technology; and teaching at the preK–12 or college level, to name a few.

What Can You Do With an Ed.D.?

The curricula that you will learn while completing the Ed.D. can also be transferable to other disciplines, such as corporate administration and leadership, hospital/health-care administration, not-for-profit organizations, corporate training, research and development, recruitment, and public relations, to name a few.

The findings from Ed.D. studies have become the cornerstone of greatness. For example, Lester Rounds's doctoral dissertation (1954) was the foundation for the development of Rockland Community College in Ramapo, New York. Likewise, William Hagengy's dissertation (1945) laid the groundwork for the question-and-answer format of *School Law* (2020, p. xix), which is in its 38th edition and is published annually by LexisNexis. As you know, many authors have used the essence of their dissertation research to write textbooks and practitioners' books.

Here's another interesting point: Completing a doctorate (whether an Ed.D. or a Ph.D.) can also lead to altruistic careers. In fact, it is fairly common for those with doctorates to accept positions where they may earn less money than if they had stayed on their current career path. Why is that, you ask? As we mentioned before, your thinking will change. You will become more aware that success is not measured in dollars and cents, but rather in how you serve others; that is, opening your life to servant leadership. You will become known for your "passion and purpose, for your questioning and listening, and for your integrity, respect, and courage" (Berkowicz & Myers, May 15, 2018, *EdWeek blog*).

One last thing about earning a doctoral degree: it is important **what** you do with it after achieving the "Dr." title. Having a title just to get a better reservation in a restaurant is not why one completes this degree. Along with the conferring of the doctoral degree comes the responsibility to give back for the betterment of society. You should be seen as an expert in your field. Start looking for conferences in your area of expertise as a potential presenter.

Apply for leadership positions in state- and national-level associations. Look for opportunities to participate in policy development at the state education department. Above all, you want to be respected for your knowledge; your name should mean something.

PREPARING FOR PART II: THE DISSERTATION FORMAT

"The Dissertation Format," part II of this book, thoroughly describes chapters 1, 2, 3, 4, and 5 of your dissertation. After this information is presented, you will find information on how to write the reference list, the appendix, the title page, the sign-off page, the table of contents (including a list of tables and list of figures), the abstract page, the acknowledgment page, and the dedication (if desired).

Before you attempt to entice a professor to chair your dissertation committee, give some thought to your topic and focus. Here are some preliminary steps that will prepare you for the initial meeting with a potential chair. Having your tentative topic, title, abstract/keywords, and a theoretical model/conceptual framework on a sheet of paper will show a professor your intent and commitment to completing your dissertation in a timely manner.

How Do You Choose a Topic? What Is Your Passion?

Most probably you have already begun exploring a topic. It is advised to choose a topic that is near and dear to you, as it will paint who you are for many years to come. You can choose a topic that aligns with the work that you are presently doing at your school or organization. Or you can choose a topic that has nothing to do with your job, but is something you feel needs to be better understood. Or maybe you choose a topic that pushes you forward, closer to the position that you wish to have in the future. In any case, choose something that you are passionate about. It is also important to choose a topic for your dissertation that can be completed in your lifetime. (Actually, we want you to complete it within a year or two.)

How Do You Choose a Title?

Simple is usually best for a title. Here is an example of two titles for the same dissertation. Which title do you like better?

Suggestion 1: *The Impact of Covid-19 Forcing Remote Learning on Academic Achievement on Elementary Students in a Rural School District Using a Case Study Approach.*

Suggestion 2: *Remote Learning on Academic Achievement Post Covid-19.*

Although suggestion 1 clarifies keywords of the study, suggestion 2 quickly summarizes the main issue. Try to select the best title; appreciate suggestions from your committee.

When Do You Need to Write an Abstract?

Your topic, title, and abstract are probably going to be the first thing that motivates a professor to agree to be your dissertation chair. Your **preliminary** abstract should quickly tell what your study is about. After reading it, professors will decide whether or not to participate on your dissertation committee.

As you work your way through the dissertation process, your abstract takes on a new role. The structure of your abstract should mirror the order of your dissertation. At the **proposal hearing**, your abstract is handed to your audience (faculty, students, and guests). You will be asked to submit an abstract with your proposal, even though it does not yet include your findings or your conclusion.

At the **dissertation defense**, your abstract becomes what is published, along with your full dissertation. You will have to revise your abstract for your defense for your committee, as well as to share with others who wish to attend your public defense. Make sure that your verb tenses are in the past, reflecting your completed study.

How Do You Choose Keywords for the Abstract?

Your keywords give you the opportunity to highlight your research variables. Keywords are words or concepts that quickly tell the reader the main catchwords or phrases of your study. Using the nouns in your research questions or hypotheses will help you select the most important keywords. Generally speaking, use no more than five keywords. According to APA, you should italicize, capitalize, and tab 0.5 (indent like a normal paragraph) *Keywords*, with a colon after it. More details are provided in part III (see Abstract, part III, chapter 11, p. 111–112). An example of keywords is the following:

Keywords: motivation, job satisfaction, teachers, achievement

You will want to recognize the power of your keywords. Google Keyword Planner (free), Keyword Surfer, and other sales tools underscore the importance of how keywords help people navigate the Internet to give **immediate access** to what they are searching for. Databases, library journals, and news articles use keywords to find references. The keywords that you select are how others will be able to gain access to your dissertation on the World Wide Web. Be sure to add keywords to your abstract for your proposal hearing. These can be revised to highlight your findings after your study is completed.

How Do You Begin to Find a Theoretical Model/Conceptual Framework?

You will be asked to speak to the theoretical model/conceptual framework you are using. We suggest that you begin to build a library of models. It will help you in your conceptual thinking. The model/framework that you choose will direct your research study. Your problem statement, your research questions, and the literature review will aid in your thinking. What are your key concepts? You can borrow theoretical models from the literature or you can create your own model. In either case, you will be asked to thoroughly describe the model/framework that you are using.

Hint: When reading other studies, keep index cards next to you (or a preferred software) to jot down the title/author of the study, the date, the method, and the framework used.

When Do You Choose the Chair of Your Dissertation Committee?

Once you have (a) a better understanding of your potential topic and title, (b) a basic review of the literature in your area of interest, (c) a simple summary (abstract/keywords) of what your study might be, and (d) a glimmer of what theoretical model/conceptual framework you might use, **you are ready** to search out a chair for your dissertation. This shows to your potential chair that you are serious and a self-starter.

No matter what the policy of your university is regarding getting a chair, it is best to start early investigating what chairs are available: find one who gets their students through in a timely fashion, who has good rapport with their students, and hopefully, who knows your work ethic. You will want to begin a dialogue with them, just as a feeler, but obviously no commitment yet, as you do not have your topic crystallized. You will want to read their publications to find out if there is an opportunity to follow up with their research.

How Do You Choose the *Right* Chair?

A dissertation chair (guide or advisor) will supervise your dissertation committee. If you are lucky, this person will give you many hours of guidance throughout the dissertation process. This is like a marriage; you have to "live" with this person for a few years.

A few pointers follow for selecting a chair:

- Choose someone who is known in your field, knows your topic well, and will bring respect to your final product.
- Choose someone who can dedicate the time that you will need to move forward in your process.

- Choose someone who will give feedback within two weeks.
- Choose someone who has tenure or will still be at the university in four or five years when you are ready to defend.
- Choose someone who commits to being at the university for the next four to five years, one who is not retiring soon or has not applied to another university.
- See if the university has a list of faculty, the work that they have done, and their area of expertise.

Most of all, choose someone who respects you, and feels that you have the ability to complete the dissertation process within the allotted time. This often may be a professor who has taught one of your doctoral classes and knows your work. This could be someone who knows how to guide you, even if the professor does not know your discipline well. You may find it difficult to find a chair because those who can chair are already overextended and not able to chair any new committees; however, they may be willing to serve as a committee member. Ask faculty if they can suggest other faculty in your department or even other departments that may be able to help move you forward.

Is It Possible to Choose the Dream Committee?

Yes, it is, but you have much to take into consideration. It has been said that when you and your chair are creating your committee, perhaps the following may help in your decisions:

- How many members are required for your committee (check doctoral handbook)?
- Is there someone who you feel has always aligned with your thinking?
- Are there some professors who work best together to keep your process moving forward smoothly?
- Is there balance on your committee in terms of areas of expertise (one who is good with developing your ideas and leads you to completion in a timely manner, one who knows the literature well, and one who is strong in research methodology/statistics)?
- Have you "earned" the Dream Committee? Have you done exceptional coursework to be recognized as one who completes projects in a timely manner? Have you earned professors' approval for your critical thinking ability? Have you shown that you are willing to submit quality papers that demonstrate knowledge and skills in the writing process, including attention to spelling, grammar, and APA style?

Submit a summary (abstract) of your topic, as mentioned before. Those who are considering advising you through the dissertation process will want a short paper on the topic you are exploring and what problem exists that you wish to study. They may also want a summary of recent studies in your area. Don't be surprised if your chair says that they don't like your topic and want you to change it. They may see that the value of your topic today may not have importance tomorrow. They could see that it may not be approved by IRB because of the sample needed (vulnerable population), exposure to a particular group (potential lawsuit or bad publicity), or ethical considerations (personal gain).

HINT: You never tell your chair when it is time for you to defend or when it is time for you to move on to another chapter. You are being guided by your chair for a reason. You are asking permission to "Join the Club." Your chair is the presiding officer of your study. This process is not democratic. You have minimal control because you do not have your doctorate. That means you listen to your chair, you don't antagonize your chair, you don't threaten your chair. Otherwise, you may hear these words: "Get yourself another chair."

Your chair (or your committee) does not work for you. They are taking on the responsibility of mentoring a fledgling doctoral student. Patience is needed all around. Hard work in a timely manner is demanded from you. When a chair expects you to submit a revision in two weeks, you need to complete the revision and resubmit it in less than two weeks. This is no joke. This is how the process works if you want to complete your dissertation within a reasonable time frame. No matter when the revision is expected, you need to keep pace and make sure to resubmit within two weeks to your chair. If you don't, other students/professors will claim your chair's time; your work will be moved to the back burner.

How Do You Start Each Chapter?

Every chapter should begin with an introductory paragraph or section that states the purpose of the chapter. Also, each paragraph has to transition to the next paragraph, allowing the reader to follow your logic.

Do not be afraid to write key phrases, even if they are not full sentences. Just get started. You can always go back and refine your writing. You will find that the more you know about your topic, the clearer your thoughts will become.

THE PRÉCIS OR THE COMPS? WHICH ARE YOU REQUIRED TO DO?

Prior to writing your dissertation, you may be required to write a précis or take the department's comprehensive exam(s). No matter which one your

A SPIRITUAL JOURNEY

As you begin your doctoral journey,
You also are embarking on your spiritual journey.

Think about it.

How many times have you asked a higher power
To help you find an article or book to push you forward?

How many times have you prayed, when you submit a draft,
That your dissertation chair would like what you wrote?

How many times have you prayed
That your committee would work well together?

How many times have you prayed
That you would pass your comprehensive exams?

How many times have you prayed
That you would pass your dissertation proposal hearing?

How many times have you prayed
That your IRB application would be accepted right away?

How many times have you prayed
That you would have enough respondents returning your survey?

How many times have you prayed
That you would understand how to use statistical software?

How many times have you prayed
That you would pass your dissertation defense without revision?

How many times have you prayed
That you would be called "Doctor?"

(Do you see a pattern here?)

YOU CAN DO IT!

Figure 3.1. A Spiritual Journey. *Jan Hammond and Paula Lester.*

department requires, we know this requirement will feel overwhelming. Trust us. Preparation, perseverance, and strict attention to academic literature will secure your ability to pass this hurdle.

What Is a Précis?

We have noticed that many of the Ed.D. programs, in lieu of doctoral comprehensive exams, are having their students write a précis. A précis is a summary of a larger work, focusing on the central points. In preparation for completing your dissertation, a department may require doctoral students to write a brief synopsis (précis) with sections that align with your dissertation chapters, such as discussion of the issue, literature review, and methodology. If your chair asks for a précis, you now know what it means.

What Are the "Comps?"

You must pass your department's comprehensive exams, affectionately called "comps," before you can have your dissertation proposal hearing. The comps are used to confirm your adeptness and readiness to begin a research study under the tutelage of the university you attend.

II

THE DISSERTATION FORMAT

Part II covers the entire dissertation format, including helpful hints and examples. Key aspects of chapters 1, 2, 3, 4, and 5 are described in easy-to-understand detail to guide you through this complicated process. Additional sections of the dissertation, including references, appendix, title, abstract, table of contents, and other salient information are also addressed.

4

Statement of the Problem

WRITING THE DISSERTATION: HERE WE GO!

One of the most difficult parts of the dissertation process (and this is extremely arduous, to say the least) is to define your **statement of the problem**. Here you need to take your time and be comfortable with re-writing and re-writing this section multiple times before it becomes crystal clear. You may want to begin searching the literature on your topic to clarify your vision. Once you are ready to begin this chapter, you may want to start with a historical overview of your topic and the issues surrounding it.

While drafting this section, think about your passion. What excites you? Why are you studying this area of research? What is your interest? What experiences—either through observations or through your reading—have prompted your interest in this topic? Is there a topic that is currently in the news that needs to be further studied? Is there an area to study that will help advance your knowledge in a desired future career? How does your research make a contribution to the education field? What resources do you have to help you complete your study in this area?

IDENTIFYING THE PROBLEM

After selecting a broad topic, you now need to narrow it down to a specific problem. What are the issues that are swirling in your head as you are driving home from work? What situation happens over and over again that consumes your thinking while taking the bus to your university? Since a topic has many problems that could possibly be studied, your challenge is to select a single unique problem. Easier said than done. You will often hear your chair say, "like finding a needle in a haystack." This means that much thought, much reading, and much "scribbling" needs to happen for this section to be clear and crisp. Be patient.

What Does It Mean to Prioritize the Problem?

To further crystalize your choice of topic, think about potential topics and research each one and rate them (1, 2, or 3) using the bolded questions below:

1 = not a good topic,
2 = somewhat of a good topic, or
3 = very good topic.

(a) **Is It Relevant?** Determine if this is an important area to study. Why? What does it have to do with today's needs—today's population—today's world? If it is not relevant, it is probably not worth studying. RATE IT 1, 2, or 3.
(b) **Has It Been Studied Before?** Has anyone else looked at this problem and studied it? Then what is your contribution? RATE IT 1, 2, or 3.
(c) **Is It Feasible?** Can you complete this specific area of study within a reasonable amount of time? Can you complete it in two years or will it take 20 years? Do you have the resources? RATE IT 1, 2, or 3.
(d) **Is It Accepted Ethically?** Cultural and social sensitivity must be considered to not harm the subjects while carrying out your research. Are you able to get full consent to advance your study? RATE IT 1, 2, or 3.

How Do You Write the Statement of the Problem?

Okay, we know this is difficult. There are most likely several problems in any given topic. What is the problem for which you are searching to find an answer? At this point, you may want to state the problem in either a statement or a question form. You are giving clear focus to your research. Examples below should help you in clarifying your statement.

It is best to first write a simple problem statement. Start with a sentence. Then, try to fine-tune it. A paragraph should suffice. Once completed, you can always expand your thinking to clarify the issue. Here are some simple examples:

Example: **The Impact of iPads on Kindergartners' Academic Success.** Kindergarten children who have used an iPad prior to enrolling in school are able to read more sight words by mid-year than those who never had iPad experience.

Example: **The Impact of Racial Profiling on Minority Males.** Teachers who show a bias toward minorities regarding their ability to learn may attribute their bias to boys of color having difficulty learning to read when compared to white peers.

What Should the Description of the Statement of the Problem Include?

The Statement of the Problem should include

(a) a brief description of social-economic and cultural norms and perhaps a few issues relevant to the problem;
(b) a concise description of the problem—who is impacted, location, field, etc.;
(c) the major factors that impact the environment where the problem occurs; and
(d) the concepts that are relevant to the problem.

IDENTIFYING THE PURPOSE OF THE STUDY

In your chapter 1, you now need to identify the **purpose** of your study, which will be an outgrowth of your problem statement. The purpose of your study includes:

(a) **focus** on what specifically your study will address and will not address (the scope of your study) based upon the problem that you previously identified;
(b) **who** will participate in the study; and
(c) **what** you hope to find (see example below).

Example: "**The purpose of this study** is to identify the naturally emerging roles of technology brokers and technology leaders in the social networks of three independent schools and to examine the power and influence of these leaders and brokers based on their technical expertise and social capital" (Velastegui, 2013, p. 20).

So, using the above example, the purpose of the researcher's study addresses the following:

(a) the **focus of her study** is to *identify the naturally emerging roles*;
(b) the **who of her study** are *technology brokers and technology leaders in the social networks of three independent schools*; and

(c) the **what of her study** is *to examine the power and influence of these leaders and brokers based on their technical expertise and social capital.*

CONSTRUCTING A THEORETICAL MODEL/CONCEPTUAL FRAMEWORK

Your study should be based on a theoretical construct (model/framework), which, in other words, should be built on interrelated concepts, helping to determine what statistical relationships you will be looking for and measuring in your study. When you were writing your literature review, you should have been thinking about a key model or concept that you would want to test in your study for greater understanding.

For example, if your study is on motivation and elementary teachers, you may be looking at models such as Hierarchy of Needs (Maslow, 1943) and Theory X & Theory Y (McGregor, 1960). Perhaps one or more of these models may be used to support your theoretical construct; or you may develop your own model (which is usually required in Ph.D. dissertations). The model that you choose serves as a theoretical foundation for your study.

However you develop your theoretical model/conceptual framework for chapter 1 (Statement of the Problem), it still needs to be fully cited, even though you may want to cite in another chapter. There are some excellent books to guide you more fully on model building, such as *Theory Construction and Model Building Skills* (Jaccard & Jacoby, 2020), *Theory Building* (Dubin, 1978), and *Theory Building in Applied Disciplines* (Swanson & Chermack, 2013), which is a short handbook (29 pages) that may guide you well. You will want to peruse Amazon and publishers' websites to get free access to previews and sample chapters.

RESEARCH QUESTION: WHY IS THE SKY HIGH?

As you have learned by now, writing a research question (RQ) can bring you to such frustration that you are READY TO QUIT the dissertation process. Have no fear, we are here (We're not Mighty Mouse, but good enough for your success with this process!).

What Is a Research Question (RQ)?

Some Starting Phrases for RQ:

- What factors. . .
- How do. . .
- Why are. . .
- Which areas. . .
- To what degree. . .

A research question is a question clearly stated that guides the research study. First, understand that dissertations begin with a basic problem. Here are a few guiding principles to remember when developing your research questions:

- Is it relevant to the problem you are trying to solve?
- Is it stated in a way that can be written in a solvable way?
- Is it clear and articulated well for the reader to understand?
- Is it written without bias or a leading point of view?
- Are the terms clearly defined?
- Is your literature review aligned with the problem you are trying to solve?
- Thinking of your final chapter, is it one that leads to a conclusion?

How do we as the human race go about solving a problem? Your quest may be led by a research question. You will be asked to define a relationship that may answer these questions: Why do. . .? How does. . .? What factors. . .? and the like. Here are some RQ examples (RQ1–RQ5) from our former doctoral students:

RQ1: "What admissions criteria best predict that New York State associate degree nursing (ADN) program applicants will enter into the nursing profession?" (Kellner, 2019, p. 44).

RQ2: "In what ways do paraeducators experience role conflict within their positions?" (Berger, 2014, p. 52).

RQ3: "How would school-related factors influence the decision of experienced teachers in New York State who work in well-performing schools, to accept a position in a low-performing school?" (Chagares, 2016, p. 53).

RQ4: "To what extent, if any, are all three school supports (instructional schedules, teaming, and common planning time) found to exist simultaneously in a New York State middle school categorized as having an average need/resource capacity?" (Corey, 2015, p. 52).

More explicit examples. You will sometimes find that you need to be more explicit in defining your research question, such as the example below:

RQ5: "What relationship exists between fourth-grade elementary school students' artistic judgment dimensions (color, form, line, shape, space, texture, and value) and their demographic backgrounds (ethnicity, gender, academic ability, and socioeconomic status)?" (Beck, 2014, p. 60).

What Are Some Common Pitfalls in Writing Research Questions?

***Do* have all RQs align with purpose.** Most likely, you will have more than one question, depending upon the nature of your study and what your committee supports. If so, make sure that the questions align to the purpose of your study and that they do not bring you beyond your study.

***Don't* have a yes/no research question.** First, you need to make sure that your question cannot be answered by a simple yes or no.

***Do* write with clarity that a 12-year-old could understand.** Your research question needs to be written in simple language so that most people would be able to comprehend what you are studying.

***Do* have RQs measurable or solvable in some way.** Since you are looking at the relationship(s) between variables, you will want to be able to measure or justify the strength of that relationship based upon your survey results or interview responses.

***Do* have your research question *doable*.** This is why you need to narrow the scope of your study. Often students come to us with either (a) research questions that are too broad in scope and will take years to study as well as need significant resources (e.g., What impact does car pollution have on the air quality of New York City?) or (b) research questions that are too complex to finish within a few years (e.g., What is the relationship between smoking and one's life span?). We want you to finish before you turn 100 years of age and before your committee is no longer at the university.

WRITING A HYPOTHESIS

Many of you, particularly those choosing a **quantitative** method, will be writing hypotheses. These are statements that are always quantitative and need to be measurable. Hypotheses should be written clearly and succinctly. They must be written in a way that allows the researcher to prove or disprove their implications or logical consequences.

A hypothesis is a statement that can be scientifically tested, allowing you to make rational decisions about different claims. We can formulate a hypothesis to see what will happen (or what can be expected to happen) under certain circumstances. Your focus is to prove/disprove the null hypothesis (H0). It needs to be simple so that collected data support (or do not support) it. Remember, if your findings negate your hypothesis or you are not able to prove it, you still have found something.

They should be written only after you have exhausted your literature review to make sure that you are not duplicating (rather than replicating, which is different) something that has already been studied and proven by others. A research question may lead you to a hypothesis. A research question such as *Why is the sky high?* may lead to developing a hypothesis.

The purpose of a hypothesis is **to make a prediction** of why something happens or why it may happen in the future, and then seek to see if it is a viable hypothesis.

Here are two examples of hypotheses from one of our student's dissertations:

Positive statement: "RtI will increase teacher satisfaction with feedback received on work from supervisors" (Zahedi, 2010, p. 39).

To show that negative statements can also be used effectively, here is another follow-up hypothesis from the same dissertation:

Negative statement: "Teachers will report less satisfaction as a result of the increased time spent in meetings and co-planning with colleagues" (Zahedi, 2010, p. 39).

DEFINITIONS OF TERMS

Your research will have several terms that have specific meaning for your study. In your chapter 1 (Statement of the Problem), you will want to introduce terminology or key phrases that will guide your reader to better understand the operational definitions that *you* are using. These terms will become more apparent as you write your first three chapters.

Terms that may need to be defined are (a) words that are specific to your main topic; (b) words that could come from other fields, such as medical or business, and may have a multitude of meanings; (c) the independent, dependent, and moderating variables that need to be better explained; (d) concepts that should be clarified; and (e) anything else that would help describe the terminology used in your study.

LIMITATIONS OF THIS RESEARCH

Every study has its limitations. Because the design of your study demands a narrow focus, it requires that you limit your scope. Limitations help you develop a study that is doable, realistic, and can be completed in a reasonable amount of time. Having limitations does not mean that your study is less valuable. There is no relationship between the two.

Limitations can include restricted amount of time, number of subjects able to participate, minimal geographic locations used, selection of methodology, technological skills and access needed, and the choice of your theoretical model/conceptual framework.

EXPECTED CONTRIBUTIONS OF THIS RESEARCH

In your chapter 1 (Statement of the Problem), you are to tell your reader what contribution(s) your research will have on your field. Here you will anticipate the results of your study and the impact they will have on education. For example, the purpose of your study may be to develop and validate a new instrument (survey), passing rigorous psychometric demands, and which may make a significant contribution. Others now can use your survey in their research, without having to create and validate their own instrument, which will save considerable time.

Your literature review may be a significant contribution for the field of education because of its depth and updated additions. The methodology that you are using or the specific approach that you are using may also be a contribution. Even the choice of subjects, particularly from a more vulnerable population (such as young children), may add to the field's knowledge base.

In your chapter 5 (Discussion and Conclusion), you will most likely need to augment the benefits of your study, since you now have confirmation of its importance based upon your findings.

ORGANIZATION/PLAN OF THIS DISSERTATION

This final section of your chapter 1 (Statement of the Problem) is to be a road map (only a paragraph or two) of what to expect in the next four chapters of your dissertation. This guides the reader through the process that you followed to complete your study, focusing on your Literature Review (chapter 2), Methodology (chapter 3), Findings and Results (chapter 4), and Discussion and Conclusion (chapter 5).

CHECKLISTS TO MAKE SURE THAT YOU HAVE INCLUDED NECESSARY COMPONENTS

At the end of each of the chapters in part II of this book, we have included a checklist to help you logically and sequentially organize each chapter of your dissertation, as well as a way to make sure that you have covered the necessary components in the chapter. Also provided in the checklist are appropriate

Table 4.1. Checklist to Guide Your Statement of the Problem: Self-Evaluation

CHECKLIST FOR **CHAPTER 1: STATEMENT OF THE PROBLEM**	*SELF-RATING (1 = Not done 2 = Started 3 = Done)*	*IMPROVEMENT NEEDED*
Introduced topic to the reader, using historical overview (4–7 pages).		
Presented problem/purpose of the study with subtopics, logically using 1st/2nd/3rd-level headings (2–5 pages).		
Investigated/narrowed the scope of the purpose, who could participate, and what you might find (2–4 pages).		
Developed theoretical model/conceptual framework (1–2 pages).		
Proposed research questions (1–2 pages).		
Included definition of terms (12 pages).		
Discussed limitations of your research study (1–2 pages).		
Identified contributions/benefits of your research study (1–2 pages).		
Provided plan of your dissertation that describes the remaining chapters (1–2 pages).		

page numbers your dissertation should include in each section, in an effort to answer the question we are always asked: HOW MANY PAGES?!!!

Of course, the answer to the above question always lies with your chair and committee members. In each checklist, we are sharing the average of what students submit for their dissertation. However, depending on your study, your literature review, your methodology, and your use of tables and graphs, the number of pages could be greater than average. Hope this helps!

5

Review of the Literature

WHAT DID OTHERS DISCOVER RESEARCHING THIS TOPIC?

The purpose of the Literature Review (chapter 2) is to examine published documentation that reveals the research that has been done in the area that you are exploring. Often, this is where many doctoral students begin the foundation of their study. They may have found an interesting journal article that aligns to problems they have faced while teaching, administering, or parenting. Whatever the reason, it is important that the article got you excited to look into this area as a possible topic to explore.

To further your search for quality articles and books on your subject, you may want to follow up with the references that others have used in their research to augment the number of related studies that have been done on your topic.

The rationale of this chapter of your dissertation indicates your level of expertise and knowledge in a particular field of study to your committee (and readers), based upon the quality of the studies you present. Your organization of this chapter will be enhanced by the thematic structure you create.

Once you have identified a topic, where do you begin? Go to your university/college library website. The website will show you different ways to search. For example, you can search by journal, database, or dissertations. In addition, the librarian will also provide help in how to search for your topic.

Hint: Make an **appointment** with your research librarian. They have tons of knowledge that will save you time and effort. You are paying for this outstanding service as part of your tuition/fees. Use it!

IMPORTANCE OF DATABASES FOR YOU AS THE RESEARCHER

Databases are organized collections of information for easy and rapid retrieval using electronic access. These databases are going to be the gateway to your literature review process.

Universities may have access to more than 1,500 databases, depending upon their budgets. You can search all your university's databases or find the database you need alphabetically. You will definitely want to narrow your search to your specific area of interest (e.g., education, psychology, sociology). To refine your search, you may want to start with **keywords**, and employ the **Boolean method**, using *not, and, or*. You can also limit your search by selecting a **range of years**.

What Databases Are Useful for Writing Your Dissertation?

At this writing, there are approximately 60 databases available in the field of education. Begin by finding databases that are most often used. They may be identified by your university as "Best Bet," "Most Popular," "Top Picks," or however they are highlighted.

Key choices for educational databases are Academic Search Complete, APA PsyInfo, Chronicle of Higher Education, Education Database, Education Source, ERIC (DOE), ERIC (Ebscohost), Google Scholar, JSTOR, LexisNexis, Mental Measurements Yearbook with Tests in Print, Professional Development Database, ProQuest Central Essentials, SAGE Research Methods, Social Science Premium Collection, and Teacher Reference Center.

Databases have made the process of completing a quality dissertation much easier since the days of microfiche and going to the library to look up governmental documents, articles, books, authentic information, and the like. These days, nearly everything that is printed also has a digital print. You are very lucky! And for all who have lived through the 2020 pandemic, digital access has allowed you to continue working on your dissertation throughout that time. Here are a few databases that assist those who are getting their doctorate in education (Ed.D.).

ERIC (Education Resources Information Center). ERIC is one of the best databases to begin your search for quality articles and resources in education about your topic. It is sponsored by the Institute of Education Sciences (IES) (see http//:www.eric.ed.gov).

EBSCO Open Dissertations (Elton B. Stephens Company). EBSCO is a free open-source dissertation database with access to over 1.4 million electronic theses and dissertations from around the world, giving you videos and links to important data. It now includes the content from *American Doctoral Dissertations* (see http//:www.ebsco.com).

Google Scholar. Google Scholar allows you to find scholarly works. It also allows you to tag them, share them, and save them to your drive to read later. Through your queries, it learns your area of research and suggests articles of interest (see http://scholar.google.com).

Network Digital Library of Theses and Dissertations (NDLTD). This digital network of dissertations provides a search engine to links on digital platforms and guides the reader to electronic theses and dissertation (ETD) whether they were open sourced or not (see http://www.ndltd.org).

Open Access Theses and Dissertations (OATD). Information about dissertations and theses comes from all over the world. Over five million works are included from more than 1,100 colleges and universities globally (see https://oatd.org).

ProQuest Dissertations & Theses (PQDT). This website is essential for you to explore as you dig deeper into your research area. However, it is not free; most likely you will have to use your university library ID and password to enter into this important database (see https://search.proquest.com).

What Are Refereed Journals?

Refereed journals include those papers and articles selected for publication by experts in the fields they represent. This process is called peer review. Academic journals, also known as scholarly journals, use a refereed system of experts rather than external reviewers.

Decisions in non-refereed journals are made by their editorial staff who determine which articles are to be published. Most likely your committee will guide you toward selecting scholarly articles from peer-reviewed journals for your literature review chapter.

Peer-reviewed process. As stated above, the peer-reviewed process supports scholarly work by employing a panel of experts in the specific field it represents whose primary responsibility is to retain high standards and high quality for published articles and academic papers.

Continuously refine and update. You will want to find articles, books, papers, documents, and the like that have been published within the **last six years** that highlight the studies that have been done on the topic you are investigating. Depending on how long it takes you to complete your dissertation, you should keep your references within the six-year window. That means if it takes you seven years to complete your study, you will need to update to make it current. By the way, this is another reason why you should complete your dissertation in a timely fashion.

There will be some influential studies that are considered groundbreaking in your area of research. These are referred to as **seminal works**. The rule of thumb regarding six years or less does not apply to seminal works.

Example of a seminal work. If your topic is on motivation, "A Theory of Human Motivation" by Abraham Maslow (1943) may be a key work for you to cite. Even though it is eight decades old, its theoretical value is still recognized. It is considered a fundamental work in psychology that has guided other researchers in their search for true, significant findings. Remember, you will want to review current studies that have used this model. You will want to present both the pros and cons of those who support or argue with this theoretical concept to give a balanced and informed perspective.

How Do You Establish a File/e-file Storage System for Your Articles?

You are now looking for key articles. Don't wait to organize them. Start a system now. Once you cite a study, a tried-and-true method is to immediately insert the author, year, title, and publication source into your reference list at the end of your dissertation.

In this day of digital access, you will have many choices, besides the "old school" method of filing cards. It depends upon what you are comfortable with. You may start with piles of printed out articles on your floor. We've all been there. But, if you are going to review 150 articles or more, this will be too cumbersome and may cause you to stop going forward. So let's make it simple: start a system now where you copy the website link into your reference list (along with its author, year, title, and publication source/doi) (see table 5.1).

"Old School": 3 × 5 index cards. Buy a large file box and label the index cards with your topic's key headings. Then with the 3 × 5 or 5 × 7 cards, write the name of the article/author/citation info and summarize the findings.

Then in a large box that fits printed articles, use file folders (color-coded by theme may make retrieval easier) and put the topic on the index tab. Then, insert the articles that complement that topic. Now you will have full access to your articles when needed.

There are many index card systems online. You could try Index Card Software for Windows (www.indexcards.ink), Winsite (www.winsite.com), or ezdatabook (www.qpdownload.com) for an index card database, allowing for quick taking of notes and a way to store information. Some may offer free demos to determine whatever works best for you.

"New School": Digital filing systems. Our 21st-century technology gives you abundant choices to help you organize your articles. Electronic file systems can help you store documents on computer hard drives, thumb drives, the cloud, and the like. There are many software packages that can assist you in maintaining your articles virtually to make retrieval easier. Check out Dropbox, Yahoo, Google, aol.com, and others that may have systems available to you.

Remember, the **camera in your cell phone** is like a scanner. So, you can take a picture of the page(s) (articles/books) that you need and send it to your own folder in your phone or send it to your email (and do be aware of copyright infringement). Then you can organize information in Word or whatever software you are using. Here are some additional suggestions that have been useful.

- *File Maker Pro*. Very easy to use. Highly rated. Has free trial. Find a used one online.
- *eFile Cabinet* (efilecabinet.com). Free demo and online support. Starting at $15 per month; 25GB of storage.
- *Paperless Online.com*. One gigabyte for free, which may be enough for some of your files (20 contacts; $15/month for 30GB of storage).

ORGANIZING YOUR ARTICLES FOR CHAPTER 2: LITERATURE REVIEW

As you read through the massive amounts of articles and books preparing you for writing chapter 2 of your dissertation (Literature Review), perhaps the following three focal points will help structure your thoughts.

(a) **Overview.** Start out with an introduction of the breadth and depth of what your research question is studying. You will want to introduce this chapter to your readers so they can clearly understand your focus on examining key findings of those who have studied your area of interest. You will use this section to justify your study and support your understanding of what has been found previously.

(b) **Themes.** Identify themes that are emerging from research studies that have been done. This will be the substantial part of your literature review. Each theme will most likely have subthemes. You will want to compare and contrast studies, looking at their research questions, theoretical models/conceptual frameworks, and their limitations. You will also want to review the methodologies chosen, including research questions, hypotheses, research methods, sample/participants, times/locations, data collection processes, and how they analyzed their data.

Assuming that you have collected information from your articles, books, dissertations, and the like, you should now uncover key themes from salient literature that best align with your study. Organize your chapter by **themes** that support your research. You can also use a chronological format that may work better for your study. Feel free to use whatever format best presents the body of literature that demonstrates your understanding of what has been studied. It will look something like this:

- Theme One
  - Subtheme One
  - Subtheme Two
- Theme Two
  - Subtheme One
  - Subtheme Two
- Theme Three
  - Subtheme One
  - Subtheme Two
- Other themes and subthemes if needed

(c) **Summary.** And finally, summarize your review of the literature as it pertains to your study, discussing the limitations and fine-tuning your study to make sure it is original.

Hint: Use of 1st-, 2nd-, and 3rd-level headings (and more if needed) will help in transition and will provide guidance to the reader (and make your committee much happier!). This technique will show similarities and differences between studies and seminal works.

Table 5.1 below shows a sample of a matrix that may help you keep track of all publications that you used. We will use motivational theories for our example. Since we shared the idea of organizing based on themes, we will keep that emphasis.

WHY DO PEER-REVIEWED ARTICLES NEED INSTITUTIONAL REVIEW BOARD (IRB) APPROVAL?

As you are reviewing the literature on your topic, be aware if the study obtained IRB approval. Most respected journals are now requiring IRB approval before accepting an article, so their organization will not be sued. Top-tier journals need proof that the authors have met the requirements of IRB's care of human subjects. Your university requires that your study receives IRB approval to mitigate the chances that your study could lead to a lawsuit against you and your university. You will be asked to add a copy of your university's approval form to the appendix of your dissertation.

Table 5.1. Template for Organizing Research from the Literature and Citations (Hammond & Lester, 2021)

Theoretical Model/Conceptual Framework	*Year/PR**	*Summary*	*Citation (author, year, title, publication info, doi)*	*Link*
Maslow Hierarchy of Needs	2015 PR Nih	Looking at homelessness using Maslow's Hierarchy of Needs	Henwood, B. F., Derejko, K. S., Couture, J., & Padgett, D. K. (2015). Maslow and mental health recovery: a comparative study of homeless programs for adults with serious mental illness. *Administration and policy in mental health*, *42*(2), 220–28. https://doi.org/10.1007/s10488-014-0542-8	https://www.ncbi.nlm.nih.gov/pmc/articles/PMC4130906/
Alderfer ERG	2012	Looking at homeless students and their academic grades using ERG	Moore, M. (2015). Academic performance among homeless students: Exploring relationships of socioeconomic and demographic variables. *Electronic Theses and Dissertations*, 2004–2019, 700.	https://stars.library.ucf.edu/etd/700
McClelland	2012	McClelland's Theory of Needs is a content theory of motivation that builds from Maslow's and proves that people are motivated by affiliation, power, and achievement needs, depending on their level of need.	Royle, T. & Hall, A. (2012). The relationship between McClelland's theory of needs, feeling individually accountable, and informal accountability for others. *International Journal of Management and Marketing Research*, *5*(1).	http://www.theibfr2.com/RePEc/ibf/ijmmre/ijmmr-v5n1-2012/IJMMR-V5N1-2012-2.pdf

Table 5.1. *(continued)*

Theoretical Model/Conceptual Framework	*Year/PR**	*Summary*	*Citation (author, year, title, publication info, doi)*	*Link*
Vroom Expectancy Theory	2011	A process motivational theory that suggests an individual will behave or act in a certain way (they are motivated) or choose a specific behavior because of what they expect the choice will receive.	Lunenburg, F. (2011). Expectancy theory of motivation: Motivating by altering expectations. *International Journal of Management, Business, and Administration, 15*(1).	http://www.nationalforum.com/Electronic%20Journal%20Volumes/Luneneburg,%20Fred%20C%20Expectancy%20Theory%20%20Altering%20Expectations%20IJMBA%20V15%20N1%202011.pdf
Herzberg Two Factor	2012 PR NIH	Herzberg's motivational hygiene theory was developed for evaluating patient satisfaction with health care.	Bohm J. (2012). Two-factor theory—at the intersection of health care management and patient satisfaction. *ClinicoEconomics and outcomes research: CEOR, 4*, 277–85. https://doi.org/10.2147/CEOR.S29347	https://www.ncbi.nlm.nih.gov/pmc/articles/PMC3468274/

*Peer reviewed

SUMMARY OF CHAPTER 2 (LITERATURE REVIEW) LEADING TO CHAPTER 3 (METHODOLOGY)

This final section of your chapter is a brief summary (only a paragraph or two) of the literature review in chapter 2. It is time to prepare your readers for what to expect in chapter 3 (Methodology), helping them transition from what others found regarding your specific area of study to (a) the niche you want to study, (b) the research design you will use, (c) the method you will use, (d) who will be in your study, (e) the instrument you will use, (f) how you are going to collect the data, and (g) how you will analyze your research data. You will also address how you will care for the safety of the human subjects (per IRB regulations) in your study.

Table 5.2. Checklist to Guide Your Literature Review: Self-Evaluation

CHECKLIST FOR **CHAPTER 2: REVIEW OF THE LITERATURE**	*SELF-RATING (1–3; 3 = Satisfactory)*	*IMPROVEMENT NEEDED*
Transitioned reader from chapter 1 to chapter 2 using structured introduction of your study (1–2 pages).		
Exhausted (a) extant and current literature and (b) peer-reviewed studies with methodologies used as well as (c) seminal works (varies).		
Presented main themes of the topic and subthemes if needed using 1st/2nd/3rd-level headings (15–30 pages).		
Summarized literature review and how this study fills a gap, leading to chapter 3 (Methodology) (1 page).		

6

Methodology

Methodology: A **recipe** written by you that others can follow if they want to replicate or modify your study, and/or to better understand how your results were obtained, on what population, how collected, at what time, under what circumstances, using what statistical method(s), and the like.

WHO, WHAT, WHERE, WHEN, AND HOW MEASURED

The methodology chapter is the one that seems to scare most doctoral students. However, there is no reason to be concerned. You are now asked to write the *recipe* (methodology) aimed to test your research methods. In this chapter, you will share exactly what steps were taken in your research so that anyone else in the world should be able to follow the same steps with a similar population and replicate your results. In other words, if one follows your recipe step by step for a pecan pie and ends up with a chocolate pie instead, one can assume that there may be something wrong with your recipe (methodology).

If we use the four *W*s (Who, What, Where, When) and the "How Measured," this mantra (not necessarily in the same order when writing this chapter) may help you remember important headings when writing out your methodology. To explain further,

Who will you be interviewing/studying/surveying?

- Overall Population
- Sample/Participants (Subjects)

What process are you going to use to prove your research (research design)?

- Qualitative/Quantitative/Mixed Methods
- Variables/Unit of Analysis
- Research Questions/Hypotheses

Where are you conducting your research?

- Setting of the Study/Location/World Wide Web

When are you conducting your study?

- Time Frame

How Measured refers to how you are going to test your RQ/hypotheses.

- Instrument/Survey/Questionnaire/Interview Questions
- Psychometrics Characteristics
- Validity/Reliability
- Data Collection
- Data Analysis/Coding

To help you in this process, we remind you to consult your university's doctoral manual and your dissertation chair to determine which format you will follow. Sometimes, your theoretical model/conceptual framework fits better in chapter 1 (Statement of the Problem). Your chair may instruct you to include it in chapter 3 (Methodology). This flexibility also rings true for other sections. Logic (common sense) rules. Depending upon the nature of your study, the order of the sections may vary. What does not change is the order of the chapters.

LET'S GET STARTED: CHOOSING YOUR RESEARCH DESIGN

The research design of your study introduces the reader to the approach you are going to use to prove (or disprove) your research questions/hypotheses. In this first section of your chapter 3 (Methodology), your task is to identify how you will thoroughly investigate the problem you are studying as you set out to discover new facts or principles about your topic. You will share your overall outline as to how you plan to carry out such a feat.

Your research design is a logical plan that explains how you will conduct your research study. It is similar to a blueprint. Remember, you are the architect of the design of your study. However, even though you will elaborate on the design of your study, there is much to be decided by you before you can solidify the methodology section of your chapter 3. The information provided below will help you through this monumental task.

Your research design should be based on a theoretical construct (theoretical model/conceptual framework), addressing the relationship(s) you are exploring and the probability of certain actions or responses. It is in this beginning section that you will explain the fundamental construct of the study you want to test to achieve greater understanding of the problem being researched.

FORK IN THE ROAD: QUANTITATIVE, QUALITATIVE, OR BOTH?

Which Research Method Is Best?

You have to make a decision. By the time you write chapter 3 (Methodology), you must confirm which method is best for implementing your study. Should it be quantitative (driven by statistical analysis) or qualitative (driven by words, texts, observations, and media)? You could use both methods, which can be called mixed method (combination of both) or multiple method (using two of the same methods or some combination of two research projects) to support triangulation (multiple sources) of data.

As you read through the research of others, be aware of the method that the researchers selected to find answers to their research questions or to test their hypotheses. Below is a brief summary of common methods. Be aware that entire books have been written about each of these methods.

What Are Quantitative Methods?

Quantitative methods collect and analyze large amounts of data that can be statistically computed in order to make inferences from the data. Surveys, be they in person, through the mail, or via the computer, are common ways to easily collect massive amounts of data that will satisfy statistical requirements.

> *Reminder:* If you do not ask the right questions, you will not get the right answers.

There are four main types of quantitative research:

Descriptive research. "What" is answered with descriptive research, summarizing **what** (who/what) you are studying. You will describe (a) the characteristics of the population (male, age 30, college graduate, four years' teaching experience) or (b) the phenomena that you are studying (COVID-19 pandemic).

Correlational research. "How" is answered by statistically studying the relationship between two variables. This is not experimental and you are not concerned about other variables.

Quasi-Experimental research. Quasi-experimental research looks for cause-and-effect relationships, **but** without the rigor of random selection.

Experimental research. Experimental research follows a rigorous scientific approach (think Thomas Kuhn), using manipulation to establish cause-and-effect relationships among the variables. It uses a control group to confirm the hypothesis or null hypothesis.

What Are Qualitative Methods?

Qualitative methods focus on words, pictures, observations, and the like to better understand the behavior and conceptual thinking of the test subjects to make inferences from the results. The interview process is often used. Trustworthiness of your subjects and your objectivity as the researcher are critical for using a qualitative method.

Qualitative approaches. According to Creswell (2013), there are five key approaches that a researcher could use for a qualitative study:

- Narrative: experiences and collected stories from individual(s) and told in narrative form
- Phenomenological: the study of shared experiences or events from the data of several viewpoints
- Case Study: in-depth understanding of real-life cases, taking data from a multitude of sources
- Ethnography: immersing the researcher into the culture of the study to better understand emerging themes of the group
- Grounded Theory: the researcher seeks to develop an original theory grounded in data taken from the field using open, axial, and selective coding

What Is Mixed-Method Research?

As you deepen your understanding of methodology, you will also note that many dissertations use a mixed method or a multiple method. The difference can be somewhat confusing, so here are some additional thoughts.

Mixed-method research is when the researcher collects and analyzes data, combining both qualitative and quantitative approaches, integrating the findings, and making inferences based on the data.

What Is Multiple-Method Research?

Multiple-method research, also called multi-method design, is when two or more methods (usually qualitative) are used or when two or more research projects are conducted.

During the 1980s, Teachers' College (Columbia University) gave one of its doctoral cohorts the challenge to have several of the students review the leadership effectiveness of a large school district. Each student used a different method to investigate the system and completed a different study. The findings were then aligned into a multi-method study of leadership and organizations (Fliegner, 1984). If you have interest in such a method, check with your chair to see if it is suitable for you.

IDENTIFYING VARIABLES FOR YOUR STUDY

Every research study has variables that can impact the results of your study. Anything that is changeable is considered a variable. A variable can be a quantity with a number of different values. Or a variable can be an attribute identifying a thing or an idea.

How Do You Identify the Key Variables of Your Study?

The variables that you select will focus your research questions/hypotheses. For studies using a quantitative method approach, variables need to be measurable in order to be manipulated. What is it that you are measuring? Are you trying to determine if the temperature of the classroom has an effect on student performance? Then you have two variables that can change: (1) the temperature in the room and (2) the performance of students. Your study may choose to investigate "to what degree the room temperature has an effect on student performance," by manipulating the variable, which in this example is classroom temperature.

If, in the next sections, it feels like we are harping on this area of variables, it is because this has always been an area of confusion for students. Most probably if you have selected to use a quantitative method, your chair is going to ask you three things:

(a) What is your independent variable?
(b) What is your dependent variable?
(c) What is your unit of analysis?

How Do You Determine What Is the Independent Variable(s) of Your Study?

Consider the *independent variable* like a treatment (e.g., preparing for a hurricane). This is your starting point—known as a manipulation. See if there is a relationship between your treatment (independent variable) and its effect on other variables (dependent). Known as the predictive variable (predictor), an **independent variable** is studied to determine its **relationship** to a **dependent variable** (criterion). The independent variables are those factors, activities, and other phenomena that change or affect the value or level of a dependent variable.

The **independent variable** is used to investigate its effect on a dependent variable. We suggest that if you need more support, watch some YouTube videos, which will fill a day's worth of instruction on variables.

Hint: Hypotheses are tentative statements of anticipated relationships between two or more variables. The independent variable is **what you change** (manipulate), and the dependent variable is **what changes** as a result of that manipulation.

You can also think of the independent variable as the cause and the dependent variable as its effect. An independent variable is a variable whose variations do not depend on another variable but, rather, what the researcher is manipulating to determine the relationship between the independent and dependent variables.

For example, if you want to see if remote learning (distance learning) has an effect on student achievement, your independent variable is remote learning.

How Do You Determine What Is the Dependent Variable(s) of Your Study?

Once you have determined your independent variable, you want to know how it affects other variables. Your study is measuring the effect of the independent variable **on other variables**, meaning that there are *dependent variables* that will affect the efficacy (effectiveness) of the independent variable.

Dependent variables are those whose changes depend on another variable, usually the independent variable. That should mean that the value of the dependent variable will change only if the independent variable changes.

For example, if you want to see if remote learning (distance learning) has an effect on student achievement, your independent variable is remote learning **and** your dependent variable is student achievement (report card grades, state exams, SAT/PSAT, and the like).

If you are studying the relationship between the time it takes to complete a four-year college program (in this case, the x axis) and the stress it causes during those years (the y axis), you can also see if this relationship impacts males more than females (see figure 6.1).

HOW DO YOU GRAPH YOUR VARIABLES?

Do you remember x and y axes in algebra? The **independent variable** is the **one you are testing** to see if it **makes** the **dependent variable change** and to what degree. In statistics, the **independent** variable is often labeled as the **x axis**, showing how it correlates to a **dependent** variable, labeled as the **y axis**. In the social sciences, one could say that the dependent variable is a function of the independent variable using a formula such as $y = f(x)$, where y is the dependent variable, x is the independent variable, and f(x) is the function of the independent variable.

In figure 6.1 below, if x = number of years that students are in college completing a four-year degree, and y = stress level of college students completing a four-year degree, you can see that there is a difference in stress levels between males and females. In the first few years, stress levels seem to be similar. However, when we look at the stress level of those who are still in college in the fifth year, the female stress level goes up considerably. It is **now** up to you as the researcher to determine what that means at a deeper level. The "why" could be answered by asking qualitative questions.

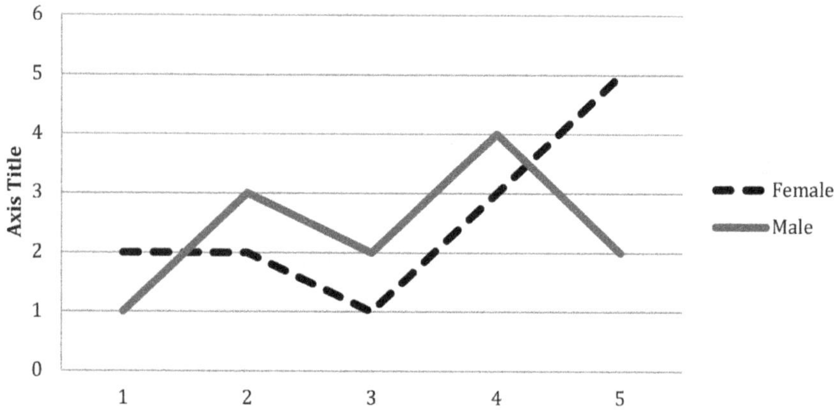

Figure 6.1. Relationship of Fifth Year and Stress on Students in a Four-Year Program. ***Jan Hammond and Paula Lester.***

What Are Other Variables That Can Affect Your Research?

Other variables that may be affecting the remote-learning experience can be age of the student, quality of technology, participation of the student, and the like. These can be considered "other variables" that can affect your independent variable.

Moderating variables. These are variables that can strengthen, weaken, or negate the relationship between the independent variable and the dependent variable. They can also change the direction of this relationship (positive or negative direction). They can be categorical (nonnumerical), such as gender, ethnicity, social class; or they can be continuous (numerical), such as height, weight, or age (see figure 6.1, comparing males to females).

Intervening variables. These are hypothetical variables such as intelligence or attitude that cannot be easily measured. They can be used as a mediating variable that impacts the relationship between independent and dependent variables. You may need to be aware of intervening variables if you are conducting a psychological experiment. For example, if you were watching a second grader complete a math worksheet to determine how long it takes for the student to add double-digit numbers, you might also instinctively be noticing intelligence, the intervening variable.

What Is Your Unit of Analysis?

Your chair will also want to know what your unit of analysis is. This will help you better define who/what is being studied. It makes you set limits/boundaries by focusing on the particular individual(s), group(s), or entities (people, places, or things/ideas) that are the major subject(s) you are studying. If you are exploring the impact of school size on student performance, your unit of analysis would be schools (large enrollment, small enrollment).

DEVELOPING YOUR TESTABLE HYPOTHESES

For those choosing to use a quantitative method, your hypotheses must be clear. They must be measurable and testable within a reasonable amount of time. Two key ways of stating your hypothesis are either (a) declarative, which is in the positive, or (b) null, which is in the negative.

What Is a Declarative Hypothesis (Alternative Hypothesis)?

In a declarative hypothesis, the relationship of the variables is stated in the positive. An example of a declarative hypothesis (H1) is, *Seventh-grade girls who are considered athletic score higher on standardized math tests than those who are not.*

What Is a Null Hypothesis (Negative Hypothesis)?

In a null hypothesis, the relationship of the variables is stated in the negative or shows no relationship. According to those that follow Popper's (1959) argument of using a null hypothesis, this hypothesis is meant to rule out what it is not. An example of a null hypothesis (H0) is, *There is no difference in math achievement between seventh-grade girls who are considered athletic and those who are not.*

SELECTING YOUR POPULATION, SAMPLE, RECRUITMENT, AND PARTICIPANTS

Now that you have your instrument (survey/interview questions) developed, you are ready to test your research questions/hypotheses, using different people or groups of people. Selecting a representative sample from the population you are studying is not always easy. Perhaps the following will help you in achieving the appropriate participants needed for your study.

What Is a Population?

Population is the entire group that includes anyone who could participate in your study. To get a better understanding of a population, the sampling method allows the researcher to save time and money by selecting a number of defined units from an overall population.

What Is a Sample?

Sampling allows you to earmark a portion of the population that aligns with the diversity of the whole. Let's use an example to help you understand the distinction between population and sample. Say you want to study the perception of female high school seniors in New York State (population) regarding their chances of getting accepted into college. You will look at their (a) family income, (b) racial background, (c) location of their home (urban, suburban, rural), and (d) age (18 years or older) to see if any of the demographics impact their perception.

Random number generator. Your chair tells you that you need 100 names for your sample, due to the fact that some responses may be incomplete or invalid. Because your sample of 200 names may be too unwieldy to manage, how are you going to reduce your sample to 100? A random number generator can be used to randomly select your sample of 100 without bias.

Using a generator found on Google or other software (or at the back of any trigonometry book), you have the ability to identify a range (in this case, 1–200). A list of random numbers will be generated for 100 names. Go through your list and select only those identified by the output of the random number generator (e.g., 3, 14, 23, 78, 156, 200, etc.). Make sure to state in your dissertation that you used a random number generator to select your sample, thereby increasing credibility of your study.

Systematic sampling. You can also use a simpler system: pick a number from 1 to10. Now count every five names or every 10 (or another number), and use that same interval until you reach the end of your sample. Those earmarked will be your new sample. Though this is less complicated, it does not strictly conform to EPSEM (equal probability of selection method) principles. Ask your chair which is okay for you to use.

Sample of convenience. Suppose you have three schools that will allow you quick access so that you can give your survey to their female high school seniors. We call that a sample of convenience. It may not be a perfect sample of the population you are studying; however, it still has worthiness and may provide important data to analyze. Your committee will need to approve your use of a sample of convenience to make sure that there is no personal relationship or bias that could cause partiality and skew the data.

Ethical acceptability. A word of caution when selecting a population and sample to be studied: Be aware of any harm that can be done to your participants. Be aware that it is easier to get your study approved by IRB if you are not (a) targeting a vulnerable population, (b) needing additional approvals from institutions that have access to the population you are studying, or (c) selecting a methodology that could cause some harm, whether it be physical or emotional, or culturally insensitive. So, it helps to use a population (students 18 or older, teachers, parents, or school leaders) that needs only exempt or expedited approval from your university's Institutional Review Board. Refer to the discussion on IRB approval (see Care of Human Subjects, pp. 87–90).

What Is Recruitment?

Be sure to find individuals who are willing to be part of your study. Needless to say, recruitment is not easy. How many times have you thrown away a survey or refused to be part of a study? That will give you an indication of what you are up against. People's time is valuable, especially during times of stress. Some people may be guarded and uncomfortable about sharing personal information that may disclose their true thinking and identity.

What tool(s) are you going to use to recruit: phone calls, personal letters, personal emails, social media, friend of a friend, or even flyers hung up in your university? You may want to offer a token incentive (e.g., a nominal monetary amount, a coffee coupon, or a gift card). Also, one option that has been used in studies requiring interviews or in pilot/panel studies is to offer a breakfast with bagels or to meet at a coffee shop and buy potential study participants coffee. You will have to disclose how you are recruiting and what incentives are being used, if any, in your IRB application.

What happens if you have started your study and do not have enough participants returning your surveys or who are not willing to be interviewed? Of course, you will discuss this with your chair immediately. Choices may include (a) widening your recruitment net, (b) reaching out to those who have already responded to ask them to share their network, and (c) revising your survey in an effort to gain greater access to participants (shortening it, putting it on the Internet, and the like). In the worst-case scenario, you may have to revise your study. If that is the case, you will have to obtain new approvals from your committee and IRB.

Whatever you do, **don't give up**. Push forward. This has happened to others in your position.

Who Are Your Participants?

You have sent your survey out to 100 female high school seniors (18 years or older) in the Hudson Valley. A total of 89 responses have been returned within the required time. Those surveys now represent your participants. You can stop recruiting at this time. If you are interviewing people or observing them, then those you are interviewing or observing are your participants. It will be the data from their surveys/interviews that will be used to analyze your results in your chapter 4 (Findings and Results).

In general, you will want to gather your participants' demographic data. Such data may assist in your analysis when you compare subgroup responses. Questions (e.g., the participant's age, gender, ethnicity, socioeconomic status, extracurricular activities, and the like) may glean valuable perspectives, giving richness and uniqueness to your study. Be sure to update your demographic data for your chapter 3 (Methodology) after analyzing your survey data (Chapter 4: Findings and Results).

SELECTING THE BEST INSTRUMENT FOR YOUR STUDY

The instrument you select is probably the most important decision you will make in your chapter 3 (Methodology). You will need to become well versed in the many ways of gathering original data to prove/disprove your research questions/hypotheses.

To select the best instrument (questionnaire/survey), you have two choices: (a) to find an instrument that has already been validated and get written permission from the original researcher or the publisher to use it for your study, or (b) to develop your own and validate it (reliability/validity) for a specific population.

How Do You Choose the Appropriate Instrument for Quantitative Research?

You will be required to defend your choice of instrument to your committee; therefore, be prepared to share what other instruments you examined. You may be asked how other instruments were used, the appropriateness for your sample, the psychometric rigor of the instrument, the data collection method applied, the coding and analysis used, and why they were not suitable for your study.

In any case, start with your research librarian who can guide you to the appropriate resources. Also, no matter which instrument you select, make sure that you have permission (from the researcher or publisher) to use it.

How Do You Use Published Surveys?

You do not have to create your own survey. You may find an excellent instrument to use from someone else's published research. Not having to develop your own instrument can save you considerable time. It is legitimate to use surveys already published, providing that you have permission. If you do not, it can be considered plagiarism and a violation of copyright law (17 USC Sect. 501–505). Be aware of copyright infringement. Also, if you modify the published survey, you must obtain written permission (and include it in your IRB application).

These days, survey instruments can be found on the Internet. You will find many instruments in handbooks, such as *Mental Measurements Yearbook, 21st edition* (Buros, 2020). It is available in print and for downloading (buros.org). A stalwart in the literature since 1938, Buros's yearbook has descriptive information of standardized tests, critical test reviews, and selections that are commercially available. They also publish *Tests in Print, 9th edition* (Anderson, Schlueter, Carlson, & Geisinger, Eds., 2016). It has a comprehensive bibliography of commercially available English-language tests and how to cite them for fields of education and psychology.

The third edition of *Handbook of Tests and Measurement in Education and the Social Sciences* (Lester et al., 2014) has over 130 instruments covering over 40 topics. Part I thoroughly reviews quantitative research methods and statistical analyses and procedures, as well as gives an introduction to qualitative and mixed-methods research designs that will be appreciated by doctoral students. Part II provides the actual surveys, original sources, reliability and validity if available, as well as access information to the author/publisher and needed references.

How Do You Create Your Own Instrument?

If you decide to create your own instrument from scratch, then you will have to document your construction of the survey in detail. Use a **panel of experts** to review your questions for reliability and validity relating to your specific research topic (searching for agreement). For example, if you give the questions to five experts, you will want at least 80 percent agreement on each question. Then, do a **pilot study** to validate your instrument. Remember, those who were part of your expert panel/pilot study cannot be used as participants in your study.

The goal is to ensure that the instrument you develop supports your research questions/hypotheses. So, you may want to develop a **cross-walk** table (matrix) that aligns your survey to research questions/hypotheses (see table 6.1) or to themes, factors, and the like (see table 6.2).

Table 6.1. Cross-walk Table Linking Research Questions/Hypotheses to Survey Questions

Research Questions (or Hypotheses)	*Q1*	*Q2*	*Q3*	*Q4*	*Q5*	*Q6*	*Q7*	*Q8*	*Q9*	*Q10*
RQ1	X	X					X		X	
RQ2			X	X			X	X		X
RQ3				X	X	X			X	

Note: Q1 . . . columns = Survey Questions; RQ1 . . . rows = Alignment with Research Questions/Hypotheses

How Do You Put Your Survey Online?

Once you have developed your survey questions using the cross-walk to align with your research questions/hypotheses, here are some survey programs that allow you to put your survey online. These programs are also good for piloting your survey.

Some are free; some give free trials (* = rated "Best Free Online Survey Tools," http://blog.hubspot.com, July 23, 2020):

- Doodle: http://www.doodle.com
- *Google Forms: http://www.google.com
- *HubSpot: http://www.hubspot.com
- Nextiva: www.nextiva.com
- *Qualtrics: http://www.qualtrics.com
- SmartSurvey: smartsurvey.co.uk
- StartQuestion: http://www.startquestion.com

Table 6.2. Cross-walk Table to Align Survey Questions to Factors

	Teacher Job Satisfaction Questionnaire (Lester, P. E., 1984)	*RQ Factors*	*Theorists*
Q1	Teaching provides me with an opportunity to advance professionally.	Advancement	(Alderfer, Herzberg)
Q6	My immediate supervisor turns one teacher against another.	Supervision	(Herzberg)
Q12	If I could earn what I earn now, I would take any job.	Pay	(Maslow)
Q17	I get along well with my colleagues.	Colleagues	(Maslow)
Q18	The administration in my school does not clearly define its policies.	Working conditions	(Herzberg)

- Survey Anyplace: http://surveyanyplace.com
- *Survey Gizmo: http://www.surveygizmo.com
- SurveyLab: http://www.surveylab.com
- *SurveyMonkey: http://www.surveymonkey.com
- *SurveyPlanet: http://www.surveyplanet.com
- *Typeform: http://www.typeform.com

How Do You Choose the Appropriate Instrument for Qualitative Research?

In order to gain valuable insight for your study, collect qualitative information (data/words/graphics/observations/memos and the like) that can be interpreted. Although the format for choosing an instrument for qualitative research may be similar to quantitative research (see "How Do You Choose the Appropriate Instrument for Quantitative Research?" above), there are major differences. Most likely you will use an interview or observation process, rather than a questionnaire/survey, for qualitative research. You may develop a storyboard for videotaping (documentary style) or for observing a classroom.

Again, we suggest you make a matrix to confirm that your interview questions (instrument) align with your research questions/hypotheses (see tables 6.1 and 6.2).

How Do You Conduct a Successful Qualitative Interview?

If you have selected the interview process as your means of collecting data from your participants, there are additional scenarios to consider prior to developing your interview questions and administering your instrument. Perhaps a *Dos and Don't* format will help you prepare for this engaging opportunity. Here are a few tips to help create a positive and rewarding moment with your participants.

Do **make sure every interview question aligns with your research questions.** This is more difficult than it seems. Be willing to delete as well as add questions as you progress in this process. Also be aware that your committee will review and suggest refinement. Table 6.3 is an example that may help you align your interview questions with your research questions.

Don't **be willing to accept the first question that comes to your mind.** Don't settle for "easiest." If you want the right information, ask the right question. Avoid yes/no questions.

Do **remember in qualitative interviews, less is more.** What does this mean? You may find that 7 to 10 questions can easily fill up 45 minutes of

Table 6.3. Aligning Interview Questions to Research Questions

RQ 1. What are the characteristics of superintendents of schools who have longevity in the position?

1. *Please share your steps in becoming a superintendent.*
   (Probe) What steps pushed you into the superintendency?
2. *Think of a difficult time in your life. How did you handle the stress?*
   (Probe) What major decision did you make during that time?
3. *If your spouse/family member(s) were to sum up your strengths, what three words would they choose?*
   (Probe) What three words would they choose if they were to sum up your weaknesses?

interviewing time. It will be your follow-up, encouraging, probing questions, allowing the person to talk more in-depth or in greater detail, that will clarify their perspective. Make very sure that the time permits you to find the richness of each participant's stories and experiences. Also, be sure to embed the most important questions within the allotted time, and **not** at the end of your time (in case you run out of time or the participant ends it).

***Do* be aware of your personal cues.** Gender and culture have much to do with this topic, even if you are on a virtual or phone call setting. So, be aware of what you are wearing, the tone of your voice, the pace of your patter (what you have already scripted), and the words that you select while developing rapport.

***Do* stay professional at all times.** This includes wearing professional attire, having your hair neat, beard trimmed, nails clean, and clothing ironed and presentable. Your nonverbal cues are also important in developing your professional decorum. And don't set up a movie date with anyone. (You laugh—it wouldn't be the first time!)

***Do* develop trust very early on.** This means that the letter of recruitment begins the trust-factor process. Setting up the interview time, whether you use the Internet, phone texting, or are face to face, is part of creating the rapport between you and your participant. Make sure to adhere to the agreed-upon time scheduled with your participant; otherwise, you lose credibility.

***Don't* use this process to develop new friendships.** Keep the interview process professional, confidential, and sincere. You are asking them to share their intimate thoughts, opinions, and experiences, which could cost them their livelihood if ever exposed incorrectly.

***Do* make sure to ask the questions without emotional emphasis.** You will want to keep your energy positive, underscoring to your participant the value of this interview for the world of research. Avoid steering the participant toward your biases.

Don't **show any personal preferences.** Stay businesslike with your entire physique, which means no raising of eyebrows, no clues of your dislikes or likes in your expression, **no shaking of your head in any direction**. Hold your papers quietly as you script any notes. Be aware of any cues such as arms folded, which could indicate boredom or indifference, or legs shaking—moving up and down.

How Do You Create the Most Conducive Interview Setting?

In this new era of pandemic, people are less apt to want to sit across from you in person. Also note that if you are meeting in person with your interviewee, you (and your participant) may be required to wear a mask, which may make it more difficult to understand one another. It may also distort the recording.

Do**, if possible, conduct the interview in a comfortable setting for your participant.** Often, the person's home or office works best. Try to minimize distractions (phone calls, emails, texting, people and children interrupting, etc.). Depending on the intimacy of your questions, determine if recording is acceptable. If you are recording the interview session, this may add additional stress for your participant. Make sure that they are comfortable with you recording the interview, whether you are face to face, recording from a phone, or using virtual conferencing. Be sure that your recorder is working properly, that the microphone is situated so that the participant's voice is clear. You will need to transcribe the entire conversation, so you may want to do a voice test first.

Do **script.** In all cases, you will want to script. This is true, whether you record or not, in case anything happens to the recording. You should also add any visual cues to your notes. Handwritten scripting is always best (no matter how bad your handwriting is) because you can easily jot incidental comments for yourself that may not be obvious from the recording (e.g., a disgusting look, a nervous pause, or a fidgeting motion). This is also an opportune time to add some coding remarks. Some researchers even sketch the room/person/artifacts to help them remember the situation.

Don't **take this process lightly.** Collection of data is critical to the merit and integrity of your study. This is the beauty of the qualitative method. The depth and detail of your participant's answers carve the rigor and value of your dissertation.

How Do You Keep the Interview on Track?

Do **be mindful that you command the interview process.** Many times you may find that you need to nudge your participant into answering the question more completely. Preparing probing questions aligned with your themes ahead of time may help in these scenarios.

Be sensitive to "wait time," as not all participants respond immediately. Sometimes you may find uncomfortable silence from your participant. In that case, you may want to move on to the next question. Be aware that time is precious.

Make sure to end your interview session on a positive note, and thank your participants for their valuable time. Remind yourself to write a thank-you note within 24 hours.

***Don't* let the participant go off on tangents.** Don't let your participants distract you and try to change your question, particularly if you are focusing on a critical area for your study. Make sure you keep control. Pay attention to time.

UNDERSTANDING RELIABILITY AND VALIDITY IN QUANTITATIVE/QUALITATIVE METHODS

Whether you choose a quantitative or qualitative method, the instrument you select must be reliable and valid. As simple as it sounds, many students get these two methods confused. So, picture this: If I am trying to hit the center of a target (testing reliability and validity) and I had eight arrows, I would want to test my reliability to make sure that they cluster. I would also want to test my content validity to make sure that the arrows hit mostly the center of the target (validating the content of my test). Figure 6.2 provides a visual representation of reliability and validity.

What Does Reliability of Your Instrument Mean?

Reliability refers to the consistency of the test (Nunnally, 1978). It is also concerned with stability (repeatability) and accuracy (dependability) (Lester et al., 2014). It is used for measuring "a set of dimensions, characteristics, behaviors, and the like" of an instrument (survey) of the research subjects (Lester et al., 2014, p. 53).

Reliability means that if you give the test today and someone else gives it again tomorrow, it should generate the same results (consistency).

For example, if your doctor takes an x-ray of you today in his office and then you decide to get a second opinion and have the x-ray administered in a local hospital, and you find that the results are the same, one could say that the x-ray is reliable.

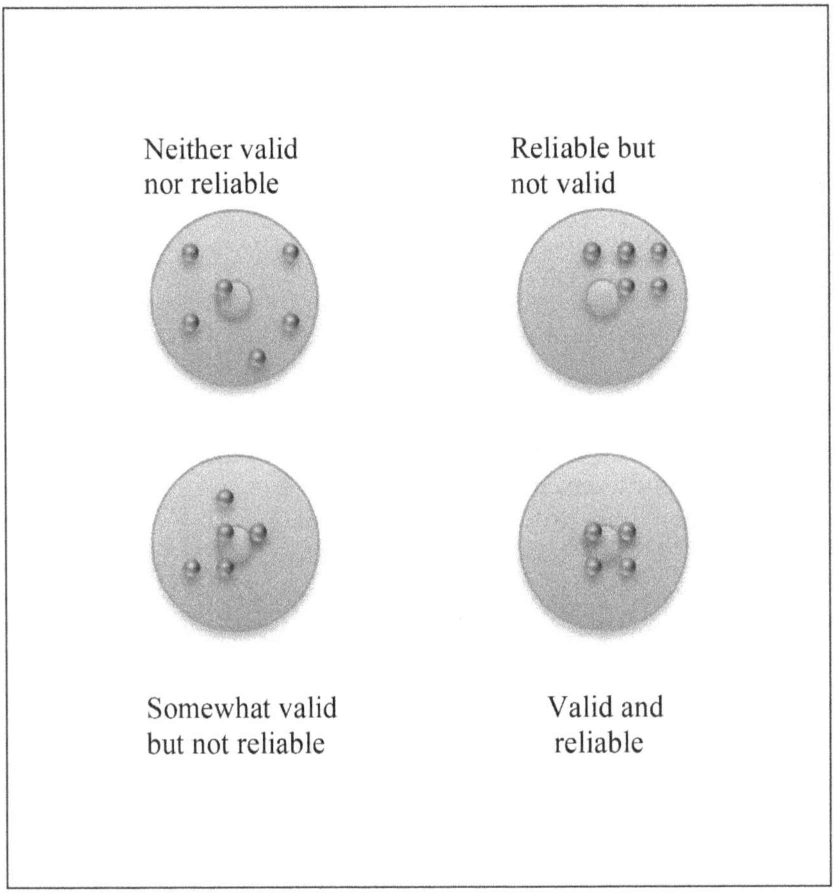

Figure 6.2. Reliability and Validity Example. ***Jan Hammond and Paula Lester.***

Reliability can also mean that it should have repeatability, meaning that over time, there is stability of the **test and retest** process. For example, a test is given to a group of students. Two to four weeks later, the same test is given again and then compared to the responses of the first test to determine reliability.

Reliability needs to be dependable. Split-half method and alternate-form method can be used to determine accuracy. Parallel forms of the same test compute the correlation coefficient to confirm reliability.

For example, standardized tests such as SATs and GREs use multiple forms to determine reliability. Tests that can be scored objectively (ordinal data) will have more reliability that those scored using subjectivity (e.g., dialogue and observations). To overcome subjectivity, often inter-rater reliability is used (frequently on essay-type test questions). This technique uses two or more raters to score the tests; then the results of the raters are compared.

One of the most widely used measures for internal consistency (relationship closeness) to determine reliability is Cronbach's alpha or coefficient alpha. This test looks at homogeneity (average of all correlations). On average, if Cronbach's alpha is 0.70, it is considered good; 0.80 is better; and 0.90 or greater is the best.

What Does Validity of Your Instrument Mean?

Validity refers to the degree to which a measure assesses what it is intended to measure.

Concurrent validity. This is used to determine the validity of a new test to how it correlates to a known test. For example, the state replaces a sixth-grade exam with a new exam to determine similar skills.

SOME BEST SOURCES FOR EXPLORING RELIABILITY AND VALIDITY:

- *Research Methods for Education*, 8th ed. (Cohen, Manion, & Morrison, 2017)
- *Empirical Foundations of Educational Research* (Sax, 1968). If you can find a used copy of this book, it is a gem.

Construct validity. This is often used by psychologists who work in areas such as intelligence, personality, and the like. It is used in tests that study formation of habits and skills. Pilot studies are often used to help support construct validity. It should have a theoretical foundation so that inferences can be made. For example, a school creates a kindergarten entry test and has the child draw a figure of a person as an indicator to determine the readiness of the child for school.

Content validity. This refers to the degree to which an instrument (test/survey) represents a specific area of content and should cover the objectives being taught. The statements should be representative of and consistent with the content of the study. It is generally established through the use of a panel of experts in the field who decide upon the appropriateness of each statement (80 percent agreement) (Lester et al., 2014, p. 52).

Criterion-related validity. There are two types of criterion-related validity. One is **predictive validity** and the other is **concurrent validity**. Both are used to determine how well a measure correlates to another.

Face validity. This refers to whether the given test appears (subjectively) to measure what it wants to measure. It does not refer to what the test is actually assessing and is the weakest form of validity. For example, when the state does not have time to determine other forms of validity, a test may be revised based on face validity.

Predictive validity. This is used to determine the future success of a particular test or a behavior. It is used to predict future behavior or skills. For example, a student gets an A on a standard vocabulary test; the following year the same student is expected to get a comparable grade.

BEGINNING YOUR DATA COLLECTION

This part can be confusing in that (a) when you present your chapters 1 (Statement of the Problem), 2 (Literature Review), and 3 (Methodology) to get your proposal approved, you have to write this section in the future tense; whereas, (b) when you have completed your study, you have to write this section in the past tense, describing in detail how you collected the data.

Remember: Data ARE always plural. (Datum is the singular word—one data point.) *Hint:* Use the "Search in Document" function on your word-processing software for "data," to make sure that the verb is plural, if appropriate.

How Will You Collect the Data for Your Study?

At your proposal hearing, your committee will want to know exactly how you plan on collecting your data. You can begin this section simply with something like, "The data that are to be collected for the purpose of this study will use the following method." You may find it useful here to use the proverbial "who, what, where, and when." A standard format may be something like this:

- Who: I will contact the principal of the school
- What: to get permission to have access to
- Where: the teachers' lounge
- When: right after school.

Obviously, you are going to embellish the above. You are detailing the implementation of your research procedure so that your committee, your IRB, and your participants have full understanding regarding how you are going to collect your data. Anticipate any obstacles during this process and be prepared to answer questions from your committee or your IRB on how you will address problems.

Your methodology will impact this section greatly. Those doing mostly a **quantitative** approach will speak to how the instrument/survey will be distributed (online, in person, mailed, and the like). Also addressed will be the beginning and concluding time for collecting the data and how the instrument is to be returned.

Those doing mostly a **qualitative** approach could speak to how the instrument/survey will be distributed (online, in person, mailed, and the like). Or, if using interviews, state how you are going to do this (in person, face to face, phone, video-conferencing, audio-conferencing, email, mail, and the like). Another way may be through the observation process (watching a video, watching teachers in classrooms, observing from afar, etc.).

Data Collection Activities. How are you going to identify those sites/people in your study? The methodological approach that you choose in your research design will have bearing upon the location (site) where you are going to collect your data and those you are studying. For example, if you use an ethnographical approach, you must identify the group or single cultural site where you will be collecting your data (see Creswell's *Qualitative Inquiry & Research Design*, 2013). Also important are

- How will you get approval for the use of the site/sample?
- How will you select a purposeful sample?
- How will you collect your data?
- How will you record your data?
- How will you resolve any field issues?
- How will you store and secure your data?

PLANNING YOUR DATA ANALYSIS

You will have a large amount of data to sort and analyze when all your results are in. So you should have **a plan** to **sort the data**, as you will most likely have a few groups (**bins**, as referred to by Miles & Huberman, 1994), to best determine where your data belong.

You should have a process to determine the **usability** and **viability** of the completed survey data/interview responses. Does it make sense? Will an empty cell disturb your calculations? For example, if the participant did not fill out the demographic question of age, does that disturb your analysis? If there are critical data missing from participants to make them a viable subject, you may have to delete that participant from your study.

You will need to determine ahead of time the process that will be used for **analysis**; that is, which data are to be **analyzed manually**, using master sheets, and/or which data are to be **computerized**, using a software program for analysis.

What Statistical Software Tools Are Available for Quantitative Methods?

So much has changed in the past two decades regarding the availability of statistical programs. Some are free; some give free trials; some may be available through your university. Your chair may have preferences on what you should use. There are two key programs that our students have used the most: SPSS and Stata. Here is a brief explanation of both:

Statistical Package for Social Sciences (SPSS) is the most widely used program by social science researchers. It was initially developed for IBM (International Business Machines) in 1968. Now called IBM SPSS, it contains statistical tools for easy statistical analysis and can be used to build models with very complex data. It can directly generate outputs into reports and is favored by those in business fields who compare its familiar look to Excel spreadsheets.

Stata, another highly respected statistical software program owned by Stata Corp., is hailed for its data management and data analysis tools. It is primarily used in econometrics and can retrieve and manipulate data. It can be used to create visual data models through graphics and is useful in cutting-edge research.

Other data analysis software that students have used for analyzing large amounts of quantitative data are Excel, Google Sheets, Hubspot, Hyperstat, and SAS/STAT (available for Windows operating systems only). You should note that Excel is included in most Microsoft Windows packages and may already be on your computer. Using the basic Microsoft Excel software, you can calculate averages, percentages, median, mode, standard deviation, as well as *t* tests. You can also get an upgrade (add-ins) for more sophisticated statistical analysis. There are several videos on YouTube to show you how to use Excel.

What Statistical Software Tools Are Available for Qualitative Methods?

CAQDAS (computer-assisted qualitative data-analysis software) offers tools for researchers using qualitative methodology that collects data that are mostly text. CAQDAS software packages are designed to aid in transcription analysis, interpretation, content analysis, grounded theory methodology, and the like.

Some CAQDAS software tools that students have researched and used are ATLAS.ti, MAXQDA, MaxStat, Nvivo, QDA Minor, Quirkos, and Raven's Eye. These programs are fairly reasonable in cost: some may be free; some may have a monthly charge. They can help the researcher manage huge amounts of qualitative data, saving considerable time and effort.

What Are New Trends in Data Analysis?

Artificial Intelligence (AI) with its unique algorithms is having a dramatic impact on how we analyze data. Natural Language Processing (NLP) is an area in computer science that helps to process unstructured data, linking the relationship between human natural languages and the computer to better understand how the human mind thinks or will think. Programs such as Tokenizer in Python, licensed under the MIT (Massachusetts Institute of Technology) license, looks at each token, which can be a word, a number, a symbol, a twitter, and makes sense of the complexities in the English language.

STATISTICS: THE WAY TO A RESEARCHER'S HEART

Most doctoral students seem to dread their statistics courses. Why is that? Perhaps they are not good in computation. Perhaps they have more of a creative mind and find the logical path to be boring. Maybe they have heard horror stories about people who found statistics to be frightening and actually stopped completing the dissertation because of their own anxiety. In any case, statistical "geniuses" have the ability to spin results into gold, simply by spinning the data. It has jokingly been said, "There are lies; there are damn lies; and then there are statistics."

So, why do we use statistics? In social sciences, we measure behavior and indicators of individuals and groups by collecting data. Statistics help to explain the data by means of analysis. Statistics (stats) are used to prove empirical evidence that supports or refutes research questions and/or hypotheses.

It will help to know the meaning of some terminology specific to the world of stats. The following are questions that we often hear that will guide you through the web of numbers.

Which Do You Mean: Vital or Mathematical?

Vital statistics deal with **averages**. They are the most familiar to you. They are most often used by the media and refer to an aggregated set of data. They are considered descriptive and used by your doctor (or insurance salesperson) when discussing your height, your weight (usually not appreciated), or the average life span you will have when compared to others (averages) from a similar population.

Mathematical statistics analyze **variations** and are the statistics less used by the media. Statistics are used to assess intelligence, assess scientific experiments, and analyze social surveys, to name a few. Statistics utilize the individual differences by examining the spread of the variation through methods: range (temperature measurements between low and high) and standard deviation (bell-shaped curve).

What Do You Need to Know About Basic Statistical Concepts?

In general, **categorical** labels (nominal-level variables) that are not numerical but are just labels, such as gender (male/female), ethnicity (based upon census definitions), and school district location (rural vs. urban), are not typically statistically manipulated (unless you make them continuous variables). Since educational studies often use nominal-level variables (e.g., gender, ethnicity, and marital status) or ordinal-level variables, such as levels of approval (e.g., excellent, very good, good, not good, and poor), we suggest you refer to a statistical text to learn more about this topic.

This is also a good time to confirm your understanding of **continuous variables**. These are mathematical variables that can have an infinite number of values between two given points, symbolized by integers (1, 2, 3, etc.) and decimals (1.1, 1.2, 1.3, etc.). Continuous variables can be every conceivable fraction (unlimited number within a range) such as weight (117.5 pounds) or height (67½ inches).

You should also be familiar with the term **discrete variables**. Discrete variables can be described as finite numbers of items, such as number of desks, rooms, or buildings. There is a plethora of statistics texts that will help clarify these terms, if you need more help.

FREQUENTLY USED STATISTICAL TESTS AND MEASUREMENTS

If you are nervous about using statistical concepts, you are in luck. There are hundreds of videos and websites online (e.g., kahnacademy.org, stattrek.com, wolframalpha.com, and youtube.com) that share how to use these tests and measures and have free or inexpensive access. We have found that most Ed.D. dissertations use similar statistical tests and measures to determine the meaning of the variation between the data or summarizing of the data.

What Are Some Important Statistical Terms You Need to Know?

The following provides a brief description of some statistical concepts and how they could be used:

Probability is one of the oldest statistical concepts, and most likely started with games of chance, such as gambling. Probability draws upon the chances and the frequency that an event will occur. Simply stated, probability is the likelihood of something happening and is presented as a ratio (from 0 to 1), often shown as a percentage (0 percent to 100 percent). Probability is used to test significance and make predictions or inferences about a certain population (e.g., in a coin toss, the probability of heads coming up more than tails).

Please note that just because an event has a high percentage of chance to occur, it does not mean that it will happen exactly as predicted. Perhaps thinking about a weather forecast is an easy way to understand this. If the weatherperson says there is a 90 percent chance (probability) that it will not rain today, you can go on your picnic. Guess what—it begins to rain! But why? Because the weatherperson predicted a 10 percent chance of rain. You lost the odds!

Statistical significance is a mathematical term used to indicate that the relationship between two or more variables did not occur by chance. Statistical significance is important to determine the efficacy of a vaccine or chances of a plane crashing.

What Are Some Key Statistical Measures You Need to Know?

One of the most common ways of measuring variables is the use of **descriptive statistics**. Descriptive statistics are used to describe the population to make it easy to compile basic data of a sample, such as achievement scores. Thinking of the bell-shaped curve, descriptive statistics use the following: (a) **mean** (average of all the numbers), (b) **median** (midpoint of all the numbers), and (c) **mode** (the numbers most often reported).

Another way of measuring variables is by studying (a) **frequencies** (reports the number of times that something occurs), (b) **range** (measures distance between largest and smallest values), and (c) **standard deviation** (sd) (measures variation or spread of scores and how they deviate from the average).

Descriptive statistical methods use tables and figures (graphs and charts) to help people understand the data that follow the researcher's arguments, leading to conclusions. These methods describe *what is* in numerical terms.

In other words, they describe a group or a phenomenon by providing a *picture* of the group using numbers. This allows decision makers, such as a superintendent or school board president, to get a better understanding of the picture by describing gender, income, educational level, ethnicity, and the makeup of the district's population in order to make decisions that may affect budgeting, curricula, hiring practices, and programs to be implemented.

Inferential statistics are used as a way of measuring the data, allowing the researcher to make inferences and forecast/predict the behavior of a population, by studying the responses from a sample. Sampling allows researchers to draw inferences from a large population to aid in forecasting its behavior based on the data drawn from the sample. An example of inferential statistics could be this: Based on my sample, I am 92 percent certain that the average age of new teachers ranges between 24 and 28 years of age.

What Are Some Scales of Measurement You Need to Know?

We use scales of measurement to capture data on surveys and questionnaires. You are already adept at using rulers to measure inches and feet of a room. You know that twelve inches always equals one foot. You also have used a measuring cup to determine how much to add to a recipe when it calls for eight ounces of water. These interval scales of measurement, such as the number of yards in a mile, are common to you. However, in research, we use some additional ways of measurement that may not be as precise. Below are scales of measurement that you should know as a researcher:

Nominal scale. This type of scale usually uses nonnumerical information (e.g., gender, ethnicity, location, political party, and the like) and is often used in qualitative research. This is used when variables do not have a particular order or ranking and have no equal intervals. Nominal information can be displayed by charts, frequency tables, or percentages to help explain data.

Ordinal scale. This type of scale has logical sequencing or ordering of its categories with distinguishable intervals between the values. Data can be ranked highest to lowest or most to least (e.g., not satisfied, somewhat satisfied, very satisfied; or when your doctor asks you to indicate pain level from a 1–10 scale), but the numbers cannot be used mathematically because of the lack of equivalency.

Interval scale. This scale, as we have noted before in this chapter, has intervals that are always standard, such as a ruler used to measure distance in inches and feet, or a measuring cup used for measuring water in ounces. The standard allows equal differences along the scale, allowing the numbers to be manipulated mathematically (Celsius, Fahrenheit, SAT scores, credit line). The zero on the scale *does not* mean that there is no property being measured (e.g., in simple terms, zero degrees Fahrenheit on a thermometer means that it represents a point on the thermometer indicating that it is cold outside). Anyone living in Minnesota knows that zero degrees is much warmer than minus 30 degrees Fahrenheit. So, on an interval scale, zero is just a point on the scale. This is important to know because in a ratio scale (see below), there is a true zero.

Ratio scale. The ratio scale possesses a true zero point, meaning that there is a total absence of the property being measured. In addition to having all of the properties of an interval scale, a ratio scale establishes equal unit points. If you can say something is twice as much as something else, such as 50 lbs are twice as many as 25 lbs, then you can use a ratio scale. This means that you can use all four mathematical operations. Ratio variables never go below zero. Some examples include height, weight, distance, money, and sales.

What Are Some Sophisticated Ways of Analyzing Data?

ANOVA (Analysis of Variance) looks at the amount of variation in the data. ANOVA can be used to look at the relationship of three or more types of variations in student achievement, such as attendance, parental support, and student report card grades, to give an overall picture.

Bayesian Approach looks at the number of times something has not occurred to determine the probability of it happening in the future. It can be used in diagnostic testing by counselors, clinicians, or practitioners.

Correlation looks at a linear relationship between two variables to see how well they fit on a straight line (one of the most widely used methods).

Factor Analysis is used to reduce complex data (many) into easier data sets, resulting in fewer numbers of factors (more manageable).

Likert Scale (pronounced lik-ert) is a widely used scale that allows deeper understanding of relationships between items on a survey. A Likert scale (often coded 1, 2, 3, 4, 5, etc.) can be used in a variety of ways (unimportant to important; least to most; cold to hot; never to always; and the like).

Pearson Chi Square Tests measure the goodness of fit, depending upon the distribution of the variables.

Pearson Product-Moment Correlation can be used to measure agreement (–1 to +1) to determine positive or negative relationships (zero = no relationship).

Pearson Phi Coefficient is used to determine whether a true dichotomy exists (binary) between two variables. It can be used with yes/no questions or true/false questions.

Rank Order Correlation (Spearman) measures the strength and direction between different rankings of two variables.

***t* Tests** are used to compare the means between two groups of data.

USING CODING TO AID IN YOUR ANALYSIS

Coding is naming or labeling something that contains an idea or information (Cohen, Manion, & Morrison, 2017). Therefore, you may use the process of coding to place the data collected into graphs as well as tables (Creswell, 2013). **Open coding** allows the researcher to attach a label to a piece of text that describes and categorizes the text (Creswell, 2013). The researcher can have a one-word identifier linking it to the question that was asked.

The researcher can use **axial coding** and **selective coding** to both categorize and select pertinent subject matter. Axial coding is used to identify relationships among the codes (labels), while selective coding is a process where one code is selected and becomes the main code (Cohen et al., 2017).

Regarding missing data (blank cells), you will probably have some questions not completed by subjects, which will leave cells blank. Check with your statistical program on how you should handle such data.

CARE OF HUMAN SUBJECTS: INSTITUTIONAL REVIEW BOARD (IRB) CERTIFICATION

Okay, once your proposal is approved, you need IRB approval. You **cannot conduct your study** until it is approved by IRB. You must submit the completed IRB application packet to your university board. They will be checking to see that (a) you have completed your IRB application in full; (b) your study will follow the federal guidelines to ensure that your study will do minimal harm to the subjects involved in the study; and (c) you have a copy of your CITI (Collaborative Institutional Training Initiative, n.d.) certification number to prove that you have completed the appropriate CITI training for protecting the safety of participants in your study.

> As of 2018, according to the Code of Federal Regulations (45 CFR 46.114 [b]) Revised Common Rule, all United States institutions are required to rely on a **single** IRB for approval for any research conducted in the United States.

What Is CITI (Collaborative Institutional Training Initiative) Training?

Your university will most likely require you to complete UCI (University of California, Irvine) human research training in order to engage in human subjects research and be listed on a UCI protocol. You must pass the online Collaborative Institutional Training Initiative (**CITI**) program (wwwcitiprogram.org).

Does CITI certification expire? Yes, as of January 2020, you must renew your certification by completing an online refresher course every three years to keep your Human Research Protection certification up to date. Without it, your research application to the IRB will not be approved.

Which Research Does Not Require IRB Approval?

"Case studies . . . generally **do not** involve systematic investigation or lead to generalizable results and, therefore, **do not** meet the definition of **research** involving human subjects and **do not require** prior IRB review and approval" (CITI website). Check with your university to see if your study aligns with this definition.

> Contact the Office for Human Research Protections (OHRP) if you have compliance issues or questions regarding protection of human subjects (866–447–4777). Office for Human Research Protections, 1101 Wootton Parkway, Suite 200, Rockville, MD 20852.

What Are Vulnerable Populations?

According to Federal Law 45 CFR 46.111(b), vulnerable subjects are those who could be coerced or could be pressured easily by those having undue influence. This includes children, prisoners, and those who are impaired or educationally disadvantaged persons, unable to make decisions. Also, pregnant women may be included in this category. If you are using subjects from any of these populations, it is quite likely that your IRB application will require a full board review. Yes, this does mean that it will probably take longer to get a response; however, it does not mean that it is impossible to have subjects from these groups as participants. Additional safeguards and follow-up may be required.

What Are the Three Categories for IRB Approval?

(a) **Exempt Category** (as of January 21, 2019). Studies requesting **Exempt** for research approval still need to obtain IRB approval; however, they are exempt from other requirements, such as annual renewal and, in some cases, informed consent. If your study is considered "minimal risk" and fits any of the sections approved for **Exempt Review** (as per 45 CFR 46), it must be submitted to the IRB and will be reviewed by one of its members (see Appendix: Exempt Status for IRB Approval in this book).

(b) **Expedited Category** (as of January 21, 2019). Those requesting **Expedited** for research approval must obtain IRB approval, but may not have to meet other requirements, such as annual renewal and, in some cases, informed consent. If your study is considered to be of "minimal risk" and fits any of the sections for **Expedited Review** (as per 45 CFR 46), it must be submitted to the IRB and will be reviewed by two or more of its members.

(c) **Full Board Review Category** (as of January 21, 2019). Those requesting **Full Board Review** for research approval must obtain IRB approval. They also need to adhere to other requirements, such as annual renewal and, in some cases, informed consent. If your study is considered to have "risks" and fits the Full Board Review category (as per 45 CFR 46), it must be submitted to the IRB and will need to be approved by a majority vote of the members.

What Should You Do While Waiting for IRB Approval?

Once your proposal (chapters 1, 2, and 3) is approved by your committee, and you have submitted your IRB application and are waiting for approval, we suggest you take the time to put chapter 3 (Methodology) into the **past tense**.

There may be other sections that need to have the tense reviewed; you are now assuming that you have completed your dissertation. (Yes, we know you have not.) We suggest you look (do a search) for words such as *will show that*. Remove the word *will* and change it to *showed that.* For example, "The participants' responses *will show that. . . .*" now becomes "The participants' responses *showed that. . . .*"

This is also a perfect time to update your literature review by searching for current studies that have been added to databases since you last wrote chapter 2 (Literature Review).

Also, now is the time to make the appropriate changes to your dissertation recommended by your committee at your proposal hearing. All of these corrections will help you move forward more quickly.

Do you want one more suggestion? We also tell our students that if time permits, start outlining chapter 4 (Findings and Results) and chapter 5 (Discussion and Conclusion). Now, you will have a much better understanding of what is needed to complete your dissertation.

SUMMARY OF CHAPTER 3 (METHODOLOGY) LEADING TO CHAPTER 4 (FINDINGS AND RESULTS)

This final section is a brief summary (only a paragraph or two) of your dissertation's chapter 3 (Methodology). Now you want to prepare your readers for what to expect in chapter 4 (Findings and Results), helping them transition from your research design (how you collected and analyzed your data) to your study's results.

Table 6.4. Checklist to Guide Your Methodology: Self-Evaluation

CHECKLIST FOR **CHAPTER 3: METHODOLOGY**	*SELF-RATING (1 = Not done 2 = Started 3 = Done)*	*IMPROVEMENT NEEDED*
Thoroughly introduce research design of your study (2–5 pages).		
Present quantitative, qualitative, or mixed-/multi-methods approach (2–4 pages).		
Identify independent variable(s), dependent variable(s), and unit of analysis (2–3 pages).		
Propose hypotheses (or research questions if not in chapter 1) (1–2 pages).		
Discuss population, sample, recruiting, and participants of your study (3–6 pages, but could be more).		
Select instrument (demographic questions and qualitative questions) (3–6 pages, but could be more).		
Justify reliability and validity, and confirm any expert panels/pilot studies done (2–4 pages).		
Describe data collection (2–4 pages).		
Describe data analysis process and coding (2–4 pages).		
Complete IRB form for protection of human subjects (1 page and put IRB acceptance letter in appendix).		
Methodology has a summary that leads to chapter 4 (1–2 pages).		

7

Findings and Results

SO MUCH DATA! HOW DO YOU GET STARTED?

This chapter typically speaks to the presentation of your findings. We tell our students that this chapter is "Just the Facts, Ma'am." This means (from the 1950s TV show *Dragnet*) that you just want to present your data. It is your job to present all the data that you collected. You are to use tables and figures (charts, graphs, diagrams, etc.) to help the reader better understand your findings.

You will want to begin by letting your reader understand what to expect in this chapter. You will take this opportunity to reintroduce your reader to what you were studying, why you were studying this area of research, and how you went about accomplishing the task you set out to do, including the statistical methods used to analyze your data.

Depending upon the structure you chose, you may want to begin this chapter with a review of your research questions/hypotheses. Within this chapter, you should share data that support (or refute) your research questions/hypotheses. Tables and figures will help to visually enhance massive amounts of data. Qualitative responses from participants will add color and richness to your findings. The alignment of quantitative data to qualitative responses will help to tell the story of the total group's thinking as well as the subgroups'.

How Do You Share Demographic Data of Your Participants?

Because you now know your participants and specific details about them, you will want to revise chapter 3 (Methodology). Your participants' demographic information can now go into your methodology chapter under the heading

"Participants." Make sure that each demographic variable is clearly defined, embedded with detail. You will also want to create a table that highlights demographics, key information, and themes.

Be sensitive to exposing identification of a participant, particularly if that person is the only one in a certain category, such as gender (only male), years of service (the only one with 45–50 years of teaching), or ethnicity (Latina).

Pseudo names are used regularly in qualitative research to secure confidentiality. Using Case #1, Case #2, and the like can get rather confusing when referring to them in the narrative in chapter 4 (Findings and Results), as well as depersonalizes them, particularly if your subjects have a distinct background that adds to the richness of their responses. In a table you can use pseudo names that align with participants' age range or year graduated from high school, level of education, ethnicity, years of service, gender, and the like (see tables 7.1 and 7.2).

We suggest that you develop a system to help you with your pseudo names that will make it easy for you (and your reader) to keep track of your participants. *Remember, the "real" list is to be kept under lock and key by you.* There are several ways to help you keep track of your participants and introduce them to your reader. Here are two suggestions:

(a) Create a pseudo name that uses **the first initial of your participant's name.**

For example, if your first case's name is **Milagros** (female, Latina, 30–35, master's degree plus, and has 12 years of teaching), you can name her "**Maria.**" Case #101 = Maria (see table 7.1).

Table 7.1. Demographic Table for Pseudo Names Using First Initial of Participant's Name

Case #	*Pseudo (real name—guard with your life!)*	*Gender*	*Ethnicity*	*Age Range*	*Education*	*Service Teaching*	*Theme (RQ)*
101	Maria (Milagros)	F	Latina	30–35	Master's Plus	12	
102	Henry (Horatio)	M	Afr Am	36–40	Post Master's	16	
103	Robert (Ronald)	M	White	25–30	Master's	1	

(b) OR you can create a pseudo name that **aligns the case number with the alphabet**. For example, Case #101 = **Alice**; Case #102 = **Brian**, and so on. (see table 7.2).

Table 7.2. Demographic Table for Pseudo Names Using First Letter of Alphabet

Case #	*Pseudo (real name—guard with your life!)*	*Gender*	*Ethnicity*	*Age Range*	*Education*	*Service Teaching*	*Theme (RQ)*
101	Alice	F	White	30–35	Master's Plus	12	
102	Brian	M	Afr Am	36–40	Post Master's	16	
103	Caesar	M	Latino	25–30	Master's	1	

USE OF TABLES AND FIGURES TO HIGHLIGHT YOUR FINDINGS

Perhaps the first place your readers will turn to will be your tables and figures. The human eye has been trained to grasp large amounts of aggregated data by observing such tables and figures. So whenever you can, you should create a table or figure to display your results, along with text to deepen the understanding for your reader.

How Do You Use Tables in Reporting Your Findings?

Tables are a convenient way to communicate data. In APA (chapter 7, pp. 199–224), there is not a section specifically for dissertations and large works. Therefore, we are sharing below the format that most dissertations follow for labeling tables.

- In the chapter that you are in, label the table (a) using the number of the chapter you are in, (b) insert a period, and then (c) assign what number the table is in the chapter. Example: 1.1, 1.2, 1.3; 4.1, 4.2, 4.3, and the like.
- On the next line, you will write the title of your table *in italics* (not bold). Capitalize the title as you normally would.

The following example (table 7.3) (Beck, 2014) shows how one could list a table demonstrating factor *Z*-scores of four different *Q-sort* models (A, B, C, D).

Here is an example of an abbreviated portion of a table from Velastigui's dissertation (table 7.4, Velastigui, 2013, p. 106).

How Do You Use Figures in Reporting Your Findings?

Charts, graphs, drawings, pictures, maps, plots, and photographs are considered **figures** (see APA, chapter 7, pp. 225–50). They are displayed for your

Table 7.3. Standard Errors for Differences in Factor *Z*-Scores (Diagonal Entries Are S.E. Within Factors) (Beck, 2014, p. 61)

Factors	*A*	*B*	*C*	*D*
A	0.18	0.20	0.24	0.22
B	0.20	0.22	0.25	0.24
C	0.24	0.25	0.28	0.27
D	0.22	0.24	0.27	0.26

Note: The standard errors for differences in factor Z-scores demonstrate cross-factor comparisons for each Q-model. Adapted from "Fourth-Grade Students' Subjective Interactions with the Seven Elements of Art: An Exploratory Case Study Using Q-methodology," by P. D. Beck, *Doctoral dissertation*, p. 152. Copyright 2014 by ProQuest (3666682).

readers to easily and quickly grasp large amounts of data. This gives new meaning to the old adage, "A picture is worth a thousand words."

According to APA, you are to label your figures accordingly:

- First line above the figure you will write **Figure 1** (or whatever number it is for you) and bold it.
- On the next line, you will write the title of your figure *in italics*. Capitalize the title as you normally would.

Table 7.4. Characteristics of Best Fit Cases for Technology Broker and Technology Leader (Velastigui, 2013)

Participant	*Technology broker reduced set*	*Betweenness score*	*Technology leader reduced set*	*In-degree score*	*Position*
Adam	ESft	5.50		9.19	Classroom teacher
Ben	gEF	4.52		10.47	Administrator
Carl	gEF	2.15		18.80	Instructional support staff
Donna	ESft	1.87	Gf	8.12	Special teacher
Emma	GesFT	1.81		1.34	Administrator
Faye		0.76	Gf	2.56	Classroom teacher
Gail		0.63	SfT	2.69	Classroom teacher

Note: G = female; E = technology era of individual receiving first baccalaureate degree after the year 1990; S = technology expert; F = formal leadership position; T = more than 24 years of teaching experience. Lowercase letters indicate the absence of the condition or a score lower on a continuous scale. Data are sorted by betweenness score in descending order. Participants were assigned pseudonyms for the purpose of this discussion.

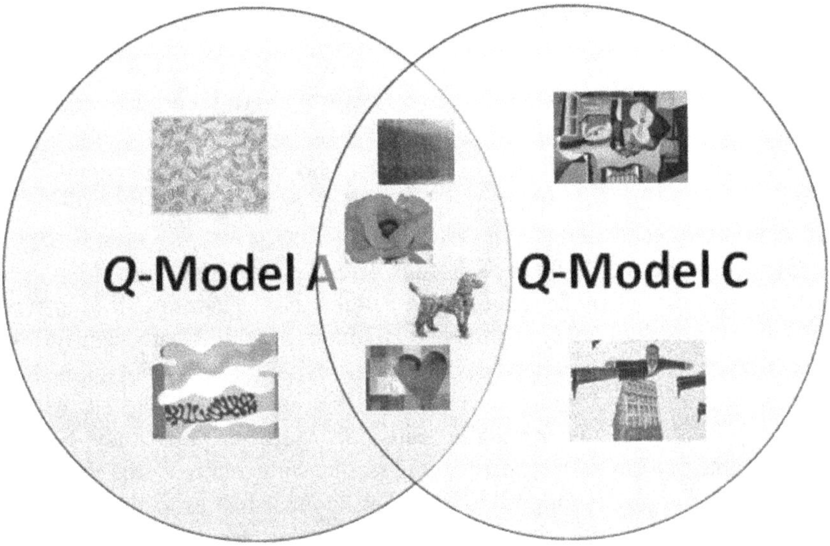

Figure 7.1. Venn Diagram of Q-Models A and C, Most Liked Works of Art Showing What Is Shared and Not Shared Among the Q-Models. *ProQuest.*

Here is an example of a figure from Beck's dissertation (see figure 7.1), showing how two *Q*-models intersect, using a Venn diagram.

How Do You Connect Data to Your Research Questions?

Research questions can structure this section by organizing data to each research question. This section will most likely be quite lengthy. Qualitative methodology is used to "tell the story." Collected data can be in the form of words, pictures, media, and the like. Quantitative data can enrich the qualitative narrative by presenting supportive statistical findings. The ability to align quantitative data with qualitative data will enhance your story and make it a true mixed-method study.

Each research question can start its own section. Here you will add direct quotes, anecdotal information (e.g., visual and auditory cues, statistical results), and other data that will answer your research questions. As always, tables and figures will drive the narrative to underscore the relationship between the data and your research question. Your collection of data, your data analysis, your codifying of data, and your statistical program(s) used are all necessary components in presenting your findings.

How Do You Connect Data to Your Hypothesis?

This is the fun part! You now have the opportunity to show how your data confirm or reject your hypothesis (assumption). To confirm or reject, you will be looking at your quantitative data to see if they show statistical significance, positively or negatively. However, you may find that there is no significant relationship. Do not fear. Your study still has merit, if aligned with the pillars of scientific research.

Generally, the null hypothesis is considered correct until there is enough evidence (statistical significance) to prove otherwise. Therefore, if your statistical program does not confirm that correlations are statistically significant, you will need to explain what that means. Null hypothesis does not imply that you are "off the hook"; you must still describe what your findings suggest.

This part of your dissertation is really the "guts" of your study. Spend considerable time and effort sharing your results with your reader. Tables and figures will visually highlight key relationships that will propel your narrative. It is your job to describe related events in detail using your quantitative findings.

Table 7.5. Checklist to Guide Your Findings and Results: Self-Evaluation

CHECKLIST FOR **CHAPTER 4: FINDINGS AND RESULTS** *(Amount of pages can vary greatly from study to study)*	*SELF-RATING* *(1 = Not done* *2 = Started* *3 = Done)*	*IMPROVEMENT NEEDED*
Summarize overall results and confirm statistical program(s)/ methods used.		
Codify sample/participants, including descriptive data, and put demographic info of participants in chapter 3 (add table or figure to represent the subjects).		
Compile findings/data analysis and results of those studied, including subgroups.		
Construct tables and figures that visually support the findings.		
Connect data to your tested hypotheses and/or your research questions.		
Share overall analysis/summary of your qualitative/quantitative results.		
Write summary of your findings and results that transition to chapter 5.		

SUMMARIZING CHAPTER 4 (FINDINGS AND RESULTS) LEADING TO CHAPTER 5 (DISCUSSION AND CONCLUSION)

This ending paragraph or two is a brief summary of what you did in your dissertation's chapter 4 (Findings and Results). Now you want to prepare your readers for what to expect in chapter 5 (Discussion and Conclusion), helping them transition from your findings to what the results infer, the implications on practice, and the impact on future research.

8

Discussion and Conclusion

This is what you have been waiting for! All of your hard work has led up to this moment. You have been on "high alert" all along and now you get feelings of losing "steam." Most high achievers have great difficulties finishing, particularly projects of value. You are not alone. This is the time "to let go" of your creation. Now you have to fight through concluding your study.

This is a joyous time. Step back and contemplate. What were the most impressive findings of your study? Was there an aha! moment? What was remarkable about your results? What was surprising? What was disappointing? Answers to these questions are a great way of writing the narrative for this chapter.

In truth, chapter 5 (Discussion and Conclusion) is often the chapter that people read first. So, in order to end on a high note, you will want to display your knowledge about your topic. The summary of your unique findings, your overall understanding of the meaning of your results, and your recommendations for the field are critical to those who may not read your entire dissertation.

WHAT YOU NEED TO KNOW ABOUT CHAPTER 5 (DISCUSSION AND CONCLUSION)

First, start with an introductory paragraph (or two) to this chapter, briefly sharing what readers will find in this chapter. For example, you can start with "This chapter discusses the findings of the study, listing all or some of the following: highlighting findings and results to research questions/hypotheses; summarizing results for subgroups; providing suggestions for policymakers and practitioners; and suggesting implications for future researchers." You may also want to include the actual limitations of the study and the benefits (impact) to the field after completing your study.

In this introductory section, you are to walk the reader through what you were studying (Chapter 1: Statement of the Problem), how you implemented your study (Chapter 3: Methodology), and *briefly* how your findings related to your initial research questions (Chapter 4: Findings and Results).

You may also wish to share how your findings differed or compared to your review of the literature (Chapter 2: Literature Review)—in other words, what results others found regarding your topic.

PRESENTING THE OVERALL RESULTS

First of all, try to avoid redundancy. There is no need to reiterate exactly what you have stated before in other chapters. The discussion and conclusion chapter (chapter 5) allows you to synthesize your results and to show how your study supports (or does not support) your research questions/hypotheses.

You should not be introducing new material, meaning that any data that were not the focus in chapter 4 (Findings and Results) should not be presented now. Your job is to accent the results of chapter 4 in a new way, making comparisons and offering suggestions that new relationships may exist.

How Do You Relate Research Questions/Hypotheses to Your Results?

A nice way to begin this section is to **highlight your themes** and demonstrate how they relate (or don't relate) to your research questions or hypotheses. Your data may have discovered themes that refute your hypotheses but offer new insights on your topic.

Review your chapter 4 (Findings and Results), then get a cup of coffee and sit back for a few minutes. You need time to reflect. Let your mind be creative. What statistically jumps out? What do the data imply? What have you really found that is unique to the field? What do you want your readers to better understand about your findings?

Quantitative hints. Digging deeper into your stats, can your analyses tell a story that needs to be written? Are you able to suggest that your data align with your research questions? Are there correlations that complement or strengthen your hypotheses? Were there significant findings as you examined the effect on each of your variables? Did your statistical methods such as regression analysis reveal surprising results? Did compiling your massive amounts of data by using factor analysis make it clearer to see the relationships between or among variables?

Qualitative hints. Dissertations that use qualitative methods or mixed methods need to synthesize the words, observations, and categorical data to create a narrative that emphasizes your findings. It is not unusual to have to write and re-write this section many times, as greater understanding emerges. Reviewing the responses of your participants and aligning their responses to your other interview questions may give you a richer meaning as to their true beliefs. Collectively, does the summary of their responses tell a new story about your topic?

What Results Are Highlighted by the Subgroups?

You will want to follow similar suggestions as stated previously, but now the focus is on your subgroups. You are going from the broad and general to the narrow and specific.

Quantitative hints. Looking at the number of participants in each subgroup, you may find certain areas are not large enough numerically to reach statistical significance. If the number does not meet the criteria for supporting generalization, it still can have worthiness. Focus on the story derived from analyzing your results. Is there meaning that you can provide the reader (positive/negative) regarding these smaller subsets? You will share these limitations when you write your narrative. Some areas may have only one or two participants, which if recorded in your dissertation, may disclose their identity. Collapsing data in appropriate categories may solve this problem and give more rigor to the findings.

Qualitative hints. Qualitative case studies with fewer participants are a good example of your need to protect their identity. You may want to rethink or collapse your categories to ensure confidentiality.

Direct quotations from your participants are an excellent way to expand on their beliefs. One structure to use participants' quotations is to align the quotations with your themes or research questions/hypotheses. This will allow the reader to clearly see the relationships between your findings and the purpose of your study.

IMPLICATIONS OF YOUR STUDY

You should divide this section into two or more parts to suggest how the results of your study can be implemented. Generally, the first category is

"Policymakers" and the second category is "Practitioners." You may want to include more categories based upon those who can benefit from your study, such as parents, stakeholders, or those in the medical field, depending on whom you wish to influence.

What Are the Implications of Your Study for Policymakers?

It is hoped that the findings of your study will influence **policymakers** in government/society who can impact legislation, regulations, and judgments (legislators/court system). Your focus is to state how you believe those who create policies can learn from your findings. You can include groups such as legislators, secretaries of education, commissioners, boards of education, governmental agencies, and other associations.

What Are the Implications of Your Study for Practitioners?

Your study may have implications for practitioners: those who will administer policies related to your topic. You will want to show how practitioners such as superintendents, school administrators, teachers, and support staff will benefit from implementing your findings.

SUGGESTIONS FOR FUTURE RESEARCHERS

Perhaps your study was with teachers; what would happen if it were conducted as a comparison study with (a) new administrators vs. veteran administrators, (b) motivated employees vs. disgruntled employees, (c) policies vs. their implementation, (d) rural vs. urban settings, or (e) students vs. parents?

Additional questions or thoughts may guide you in completing this section:

- Where did your study leave off?
- Where could it go next?
- Which groups weren't included that can be included in the next study?
- What areas of the state/country were omitted?
- Should a study now sample urban, suburban, or rural communities?
- What grade levels could be the focus next time?
- What demographic characteristics were excluded (e.g., gender, age, ethnicity)?
- How can international researchers use your study to further their inquiry?
- What fields (e.g., business management, education, law, philosophy, psychology, sociology, technology) can use your study as a springboard for their research?

LIMITATIONS AND BENEFITS OF YOUR STUDY

Every study has its **limitations**. By design, one must have a narrow scope to pinpoint the effects of causation on variables. A study cannot include everything. Time is limited. Resources are limited. Access to your committee is also limited.

Additionally, dissertations are to be completed in a timely fashion (see the manual of your university), so it stands to reason that your study will have limitations. Limitations can include conceptual framework, location, methodology, research design, subjects' demographic characteristics, timing, and the like.

Your study may "fill a gap" in the literature, thereby providing a **benefit** to others. It could have meaningful influence in your field. It could benefit future researchers who may choose to study another age group or another group of people. Other doctoral students may want to replicate your study, especially if you (a) developed an instrument that had reliability and validity, (b) used grounded theory, or (c) created a new theoretical framework.

The results of your study may take on a life of their own. Think of Lester Rounds and his dissertation (Rounds, 1954): there is now a community college in New York State that was the outgrowth of his dissertation (SUNY Rockland Community College, n.d.).

WRITING THE CONCLUDING PARAGRAPH(S) OF YOUR STUDY

This last section of your dissertation's chapter 5 is generally called "Conclusion." You will summarize how the purpose and processes of your study shed light on a new area of inquiry. In these final paragraphs, you will take this opportunity to highlight your findings and report the impact of your results.

You started this dissertation strong—now you want to end strong (see table 8.1, to make sure you covered everything that was needed).

Enjoy this moment. You have completed the arduous and academic part of this journey. Of course, you still will have to review and re-write as needed. What is left before your dissertation defense is the nitty-gritty, such as (a) cleaning up your reference list, (b) aligning your appendices, (c) putting the page numbers in your table of contents and listing your tables/graphs, and (d) addressing the other areas listed below.

You have finished the body of your dissertation. Your work is not over. Now you have to complete the (a) reference list, (b) appendix, (c) title page, (d) abstract, and (e) acknowledgment and dedication pages.

Table 8.1. Checklist to Guide Your Discussion and Conclusion: Self-Evaluation

CHECKLIST FOR **CHAPTER 5: DISCUSSION AND CONCLUSION**	*SELF-RATING (1 = Not done 2 = Started 3 = Done)*	*IMPROVEMENT NEEDED*
Present overall results, including themes and surprising findings (1–3 pages).		
Discuss summary of results as they relate to hypotheses and/or research questions (2–3 pages).		
Discuss summary of subgroup results to hypotheses and/or research questions (2–3 pages).		
Express implications for policymakers, practitioners, and others (1–2 pages).		
Suggest problems and implications for future researchers (1–2 pages).		
Share limitations and benefits of this study for the field (1–2 pages).		
Wrap up your dissertation with a concluding paragraph(s) (1–2 pages).		

9

References (Your Reference List)

The reference list is one of the most tedious and uninteresting areas, as per the comments from our students. With APA changing formats over the past year, our students are ready to pull their hair out (or whatever is left of it!). This is one of the reasons we tell our students to complete their dissertation in a timely fashion, as changes in staff, in IRB policies, and in APA format can change during the time you are working on your dissertation. You need to be flexible and be ready to adjust to changes.

Your reference list needs to comply with reference standards: you cannot just make up your own format, especially at the doctoral-degree level. Your reference list must be double spaced, as should be your entire document with no return strokes between sections; just run it continuously. Hanging indents are to be used in the reference list. You must follow the guidelines: how to cite books, articles, use of doi or URL, and the like.

Adherence to guidelines of APA (or whatever style manual your university requires) is critical to demonstrate your professional acumen. These style manuals (some are online, but a hard copy is always a must for you) are worth their weight in gold—read yours from beginning to end. Earmark and highlight areas that you should read over and over.

Most probably your most common references will be from journals. Remember, everything is alphabetical, starting with the author(s) last name. Be aware that book formats are treated differently from journals, and Internet retrieval is different from everything else! Does it have a doi? Sometimes an author's name is not listed (see p. 280 in APA 7th ed.); perhaps it is a pamphlet published by a government agency (see pp. 329–31 in APA 7th ed.), considered *gray literature* (not peer reviewed); or maybe you are using a dissertation that has not been published (see pp. 333–34 in APA 7th ed.). Have patience: you will find many scenarios to support your particular needs.

APA reminds us that each reference has four elements (see p. 283 in APA 7th ed.). They are **author**, **date**, **title**, and **source**. You will want to have handy both (a) Chapter 9: Reference List (see pp. 281–309 in APA 7th ed.) and (b) Chapter 10: Reference Examples (see pp. 313–52 in APA 7th ed.) whenever you add references to this section. If you have legal references, see Chapter 11: Legal References (see pp. 355–68 in APA 7th ed.).

Universities and other helpful sites aid in this process. Penn State University (guides.libraries.psu.edu), Purdue University's Owl (owl.purdue.edu), and Washington University (guides.lib.uw.edu) are three sites that have access 24/7. Chatting with students at owl.purdue.edu is a great way to find out how to write out your citations, whether APA, Chicago (CMOS), or MLA. Your university may also have reference aids and live chats to aid in this process. Be patient; you can and will do this successfully!

Table 9.1. Checklist to Guide Your Reference List: Self-Evaluation (According to APA 7th edition, the reference list should follow a specific format.)

CHECKLIST FOR **REFERENCE LIST** *(Using APA 7th Edition, 2020, Chapter 9 and Chapter 10. See example on pp. 66–67.)*	*SELF-RATING (1 = Not done 2 = Started 3 = Done)*	*IMPROVEMENT NEEDED*
Alphabetize by author's last name or title of reference/organization if author is not known and follow APA to a "T."		
Refer to "Periodicals," 10.1 (p. 316 in APA), and section for articles.		
Refer to "Books and Reference Works," 10.2 (p. 321 in APA), and section for books.		
Refer to "Edited Book Chapters and Entries in Reference Works," 10.3 (p. 326 in APA), for book chapters.		
Refer to chapter 10 in APA for additional reference examples.		

10

Appendix

The appendix helps you add supplemental information that supports your findings and any other pertinent, yet nonessential, information that the reader may want to know about your study. Each appendix has its own label and title. The appendix allows the narrative to flow more smoothly, without adding lengthy or unwieldy information or data. Material inserted in the appendix can include supplemental data, supportive data analysis, IRB approval/letter of informed consent, IRB approved status, survey instrument or interview questions, letters used for data collection, and data that can be shown in additional tables, graphs, diagrams, and the like. Copyrighted information, such as (a) the use of a survey instrument or questionnaire, (b) use of a theoretical model/conceptual framework from someone else's study, or (c) use of specific videos or photos that need a permission letter from the author/photographer and may also need permission from the publisher.

Appendix A (label)
Permission Letter for Participants (title)

As with other APA guidelines, specific formats and rules are to be followed (see pp. 41–43 in APA 7th ed.). Everything in the appendix must also be cited in your dissertation. Label your material in the appendix based upon the order that it was referred to in your text (e.g., Appendix A, Appendix B, Appendix C, etc.).

Additional rules that apply to the appendix section include (a) keeping the page numbers continuous in your dissertation; (b) a separate page is needed for each appendix with the first appendix beginning after the reference list; (c) the label and title are to be centered and in bold font; (d) additional tables and figures posted in the appendix need to be labeled (e.g., Table A, Table B, Table C, and the like); and (e) all appendices should be listed in your table of contents.

Table 10.1. Checklist to Guide Your Appendix: Self-Evaluation

CHECKLIST FOR **APPENDIX** *(Using APA 7th Edition, 2020. See pp. 41–43)*	*SELF-RATING (1 = Not done 2 = Started 3 = Done)*	*IMPROVEMENT NEEDED*
Appendix labels should be capitalized, centered, and bold.		
Appendix labels are ordered by A, B, C, or Table A1, A2, B1, B2, etc.		
Present each appendix label in the order in which it appears in the dissertation.		
See pages 42–43 in APA for online supplemental materials.		
Make sure to list all appendix labels and titles in your table of contents.		

11

How to Write Additional Sections

Now that you have finished the body of your dissertation, this chapter will address key information that will help you write your (a) title page, (b) Dissertation Defense Approval form, (c) abstract page, (d) acknowledgment page and dedication (if desired), and (e) table of contents section (including the list of tables and list of figures). Check with your department as to the format that is required by your college. If in doubt, review a number of dissertations that have come from your department, which most likely can be found in your library.

TITLE (COVER) PAGE

Your dissertation will begin with a title (cover) page (see pp. 31–32 in APA 7th ed.). The running head (created using the "Header/Footer" function) is a brief summary of your title (maximum of 50 characters). All letters in the header are capitalized, which will continue running throughout your paper. Page numbers (on right) will be opposite the running head (on left), beginning with page one (title page).

The title that you first choose (working title) may not be the title on your final document. The purpose of a title is to encourage others to read your document (i.e., your dissertation). So, it is necessary that your title conveys the essence of your study for anyone who looks at it by choosing appropriate words that draw upon the value of your study. Your title should be catchy yet precise and should portray the uniqueness of your study.

A colon may be used to separate phrases to entice others to read your study. An example of a title with a colon may help: "School Choice and Student

Performance: The Impact of No Child Left Behind." So, based upon this title, one who is searching for teacher satisfaction may not find this study suited to their needs.

Your title page should align with your university's dissertation requirements. See your university's doctoral manual to ensure that you are doing it correctly. Figure 11.1 is a sample from our experiences.

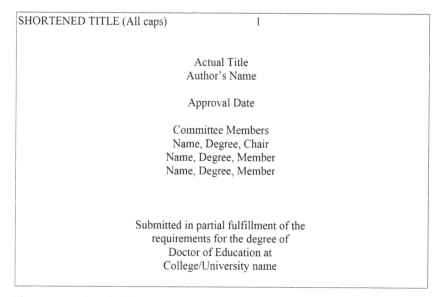

SHORTENED TITLE (All caps) 1

Actual Title
Author's Name

Approval Date

Committee Members
Name, Degree, Chair
Name, Degree, Member
Name, Degree, Member

Submitted in partial fulfillment of the
requirements for the degree of
Doctor of Education at
College/University name

Figure 11.1. Sample Title (Cover) Page. ***Jan Hammond and Paula Lester.***

DISSERTATION DEFENSE APPROVAL FORM

A critical addition to your dissertation is the sign-off form, demonstrating that you have successfully defended your dissertation. This form should be **inserted into your dissertation** (without a page number), following the title page.

This form will record your name, the title of your dissertation, the date you successfully defended, and the formal names of all committee members, with your chair's name and degree first. *Hint:* We suggest that you remind your **chair prior** to your day of defense to bring the printed form to your defense, with the signature lines blank.

This form needs to be signed on the day of your approved defense, and signed either in person or remotely by all committee members. Usually your chair will take this responsibility. It must then be submitted to the department secretary who will obtain the required additional signature(s) of the dean or director of the doctoral program. Make sure you have a copy of the page with signatures to be filed for safe keeping.

Recent policies suggest, for security's sake, that the final sign-off form with committee members' personal signatures stay with the university. Only their names, their positions on the committee, and their earned degrees are included in your published dissertation.

ABSTRACT

As indicated before, the purpose of the abstract is to showcase your dissertation. This is the first introduction to your study seen by the outside world, often found by your title and keywords. The abstract is a brief summary of your dissertation, no more than 250 words according to APA (see p. 38 in APA 7th ed.), written to entice researchers to read your whole study. It will speak to what your dissertation was about, what method and research design you used, the sample and instrument used, your analysis, your findings and results, and your conclusions. The abstract is numbered page 2; the title page is numbered page 1.

How Do You Format Your Final Abstract?

Once you have defended your dissertation, you will revise your abstract again for **final submission** to ProQuest and wherever else you submit it for public view. Write a clear, concise, accurate, and nonjudgmental account of your research. This all has to be done within 150 to 250 words, according to APA guidelines. The last line in your abstract contains your keywords. Here are some key points:

- Write **Abstract** in bold and centered on a clean page after your title page.
- Begin your paragraph flush left (not indented). Usually your abstract will be only one paragraph written in past tense (theories and the like are written in present tense).
- You can start with the statement of the problem (very short) and main issues surrounding it that led to the purpose of your study.
- You may want to speak to what other researchers found and how your study builds upon their findings, briefly discussing your theoretical model or conceptual framework.

- Readers will want to know the methodology you used, including research design, sample, location/site, instrument/survey, data collected and analyzed. (Be brief!)
- Critical to the abstract is highlighting your findings and the conclusions you have drawn.
- Keywords come at the end of your abstract. They are in a separate paragraph, indented, with *Keywords:* italicized (not bolded), capitalized, and a colon after *Keywords* (see pp. 38–39 in APA 7th ed.). Your keywords that follow the colon are not capitalized, are separated by commas, and have no period at the end. They are considered the most important words/phrases to attract people to your dissertation. Three to five keywords/phrases is the normal amount of words listed.

ACKNOWLEDGMENT AND DEDICATION PAGES (OPTIONAL)

Dedicating your hard work to a person or thing is a touching moment to whomever receives the honor. Here are some simple dedication ideas you may find useful: "This dissertation is dedicated to my husband: my best friend"; "I dedicated this dissertation to my two grandmothers." It could be someone who is no longer on earth or it could even be a favorite cat. This is your moment to decide whose name deserves this grand spot. Your gift will be cherished for a lifetime.

Your acknowledgment section is very enjoyable to write. We suggest that you do it at the end of your journey to celebrate the completion of a lifetime dream. A basic rule of thumb for this section is as follows:

First, thank your chair and each individual committee member. For the most part, their support is a way for them to "give back and pay it forward," otherwise known as a "labor of love," as the compensation (or not!) does not match the amount of time and thought they have given to you. Committee members agree to "sign up" because it is required in our field to support the next generation of researchers and to guarantee that those who earn the doctoral degree deserve it, according to the ethics of the field. Committee members are the gatekeepers to the profession.

Next, thank other faculty or professionals who inspired or supported you along your journey. You may thank the professionals as well as association/government members who gave you access to the site(s) and also give thanks to the survey participants. You may also want to thank members of your cohort or people you work with or even students or mentors who have seen you toil over the last few years.

Finally, you will get great joy in thanking your family and close friends who have been with you every step of the way.

COMPLETING YOUR TABLE OF CONTENTS, LIST OF TABLES, AND LIST OF FIGURES

Because you have to eventually put in page numbers for your table of contents, list of tables, and list of figures sections, we suggest you use a spreadsheet program to assist in this process. Once again, we recommend that you check with your university dissertation manual and your dissertation chair while completing these sections.

You will notice that in the sample table of contents (figure 11.2) below, we included the words "Introductory Paragraph(s)." This is to guide you in writing the first paragraph(s) in each chapter. You may want to use the word "Introduction" to get you started in these sections. We suggest that you write the word "Introduction," and then, once you complete the section, **remove** that heading. We have found that using "Introduction" helps our students stay focused.

In figure 11.2, we have inserted Roman numerals where your paper may use them (check with your university guidelines). We inserted the pound sign (#) where you will write the correct ordinal number.

Chances are you will have more themes or subthemes than we have listed in the example. The table of contents in figure 11.2 should help you organize your table of contents as it aligns with your study. Please note that you will also have to separately include a list of tables (see figure 11.3), followed by a list of figures (see figure 11.4).

TABLE OF CONTENTS

Figure 11.2. Sample Table of Contents. ***Jan Hammond and Paula Lester.***

LIST OF TABLES

Figure 11.3. Sample List of Tables. *Jan Hammond and Paula Lester.*

LIST OF FIGURES

Figure 11.4. Sample List of Figures. *Jan Hammond and Paula Lester.*

III

AND ALL THE OTHER STUFF

Part III reminds you that there is more to this doctoral process than just writing a dissertation. Part III helps to prepare you for your Proposal Hearing and the Dissertation Defense. University protocols and opportunities for Ed.D. graduates are also highlighted.

12

The Proposal Hearing

So, you have passed your comps, drafted your first three chapters, and now you are ready to present your topic and how you plan to implement your study. To have progressed this far in your doctoral pursuit, you have **reached a major milestone**. Take a breath and pat yourself on the back (because no one else will!).

REACHING A DEFINING MOMENT

This now **takes all of your time** to finalize your dissertation. This is the time that you must get up at 4:30 a.m. and work on your research—before you shower, feed the kids, and go to work. Once you come home, before preparing a very simple dinner (no time for making pasta from scratch or epicurean delights), you need to be at that computer, moving forward. Hopefully, everyone around you is entirely supportive. You should be in full gear with your eye on the prize (completion of your dissertation).

There are a few major hurdles you will have to overcome; never fear—you can do it. Time is of the essence. At this point, you can either complete your dissertation within a semester (rare, but doable) or within 20 years (please!). You are the captain of your ship now.

Be aware that your committee has not signed on for a lifetime contract. They could be unable to continue because of health, relocation, sabbatical, other professional commitments, retirement, or—well, let's not go there. Be cognizant of your chair's tenure at the university and anticipated longevity as your chair.

This is also a time that you need to have everything backed up in triplicate. Strange things happen for which you can't prepare. If we told you that we had students who lost their entire dissertation due to flooding (major hurricane unexpected); lightning frying their computer; destruction of their flash drive; unanticipated events such as car theft, including their laptop; leaving their laptop in an unsecured place—never to be found again; or a toddler destroying what they forgot to save, this would only be the tip of the iceberg.

Words of wisdom: Put your thumb drive with your entire study on a chain/ necklace. Have it with you wherever you go; that way, you will always have it handy in case you have a moment to work on it. Also, make sure you save constantly on the cloud. One more safety tip: When you finish each night, **send yourself a copy** via your email. These small tips will save you time and aggravation.

Let's get you started. Here are suggestions to help you successfully defend your proposal hearing.

What Do You Do in Advance of the Day of Your Proposal Hearing?

This is one time that you **must** pay attention to details and deadlines. You must follow the **doctoral handbook** precisely. There are deadlines for you to **submit copies of your proposal** to the office. A **room**, **date**, and **time** must be scheduled and approved for your hearing (typically, you will need at least an hour). The department needs time to **notify appropriate faculty** (and students, if warranted) of your hearing.

You should survey the designated room ahead of time and determine what information technology (IT) is provided and make sure that you are comfortable with it and able to use it. If additional IT support is needed, it is your responsibility to follow through, whether it be an additional extension cord, a replacement of the battery in the remote, or a place to set your laptop. Is the temperature okay? Is it dark enough so folks can see your visual slides? Are there enough chairs? If you are connecting using video conferencing, is the Internet service strong enough? If passwords are needed to get you onto areas of the Internet, make sure you have access.

Taking care of all these details will help calm your nerves and make your presentation go smoothly. There is nothing worse than coming into the room for the first time on the day of your proposal hearing—a recipe for disaster.

Your chair will most likely ask you to submit your visual slides ahead of time to your committee. Make sure to do that in a timely fashion. For those of you who are doing everything remotely, have your committee try the link prior to the day of your presentation to confirm that their Wi-Fi signal can support the video conference call.

How Long Should Your Proposal Hearing Presentation Be?

As a rule of thumb, 15 to 20 minutes is a standard amount of time for you to share your anticipated research with your committee. Your committee chair will be the one who will advise you if it is okay to be longer.

During your presentation, you will give an overview of your study, with a caveat—"If you would like me to expand on this area, I will be happy to give more detail."

After your presentation, your chair will lead the questioning session. You will answer the questions from your committee members first. Other faculty may then raise questions for you as well. Since this is a learning opportunity for students, your chair may ask if any student has a question.

You want to focus on the question that is being asked, rather than the question you wanted (which may show a lack of understanding). You certainly can ask for clarification. Remember, no one should be there to try to harm you; their intent should be to help secure quality research. Breathe. Take your time to answer carefully. There is no need to rush. Everyone who has completed their dissertation has been in the same "hot seat" that you are in now.

What Is the Best Way to Present Your First Three Chapters?

Visual presentation formats (e.g., Google Slides, Keynote, PowerPoint, Prezi, and Vizmi) will enhance your information in a visual manner so that your committee can follow your logic. Find the format that is **easiest** for you. This is not the time to experiment. Simplicity always wins in this scenario. Don't try to bluff your way through the proposal hearing, thinking that your ability to use high tech will make you shine. Going to other proposal hearings will give you a better understanding of what works best. When in doubt, check with your chair.

How Do You Organize Your Presentation?

First, you will want to prepare an outline that aligns with the main sections of your table of contents. We are always asked, How many slides for each section? Usually students have way too many slides (maybe even 40 or 50!). In truth, the slides are there only to support your patter, not to be read word for word.

When scaling down your slides to the minimum needed to present a well-organized, cogent, clear, and concise presentation, you can save the less-needed slides as supplemental material if questions arise during your proposal hearing. In general, 10 to 20 slides should be sufficient to cover your content.

The presentation can be organized in many ways. Here is a suggested format for your slides:

- **Title Slide (1 slide).** Include your title, your name, your university, date of proposal hearing, and the names of your committee members, starting with your chairperson. Make sure you spell all names correctly, with their degree after their name and the role they hold on your dissertation committee.
- **Overview of Your Topic, Research Questions, Key Terms (2–4 slides).** Include the introduction, historical background, and context of your study. Address the purpose of your study, the statement of the problem, and the theoretical model/conceptual framework. Your research questions can go here or in your methodology section. Introduce key terms that are critical for your audience to better understand the description you are using.
- **Overview of Your Literature Review (2–4 slides).** Highlight the salient literature studies that are the cornerstone to the research you are proposing. You will want to subdivide your review of the literature into **content sections** that are closely related to the context of your study. Be sure to speak to the merits and demerits (pros and cons) of their research findings. These studies should support the path that guides your study. This is a good time for you to share how your research fills a gap in the literature.
- **Overview of Your Methodology (3–5 slides).** First, address your research design, including your approach (quantitative/qualitative/mixed methods) and the procedures that you will use. You will state the population, sample, and those that qualify as participants. You will introduce the data collection method you will use, including any software or online survey programs that you may be using. You must also present the questionnaire/survey or interview questions that you will be adhering to. This is critical, because if you make changes, you must also get permission from your committee as well as IRB, if appropriate. You will need to address how you are going to analyze data and coding as required.
- **Overview of How to Protect Human Subjects/Ethical Concerns (1 slide).** On this slide, ensure that your participants will not be harmed in any way, including physically, mentally, emotionally, or professionally. You need to explain how you are going to protect confidentiality or anonymity. Participants need to be assured that they can stop the survey or interviewing process at any time without repercussions. If you are providing some form of compensation, that needs to be disclosed. If there are any emotional ramifications for the participants during or after

their participation, tell your committee what action(s) you would take to secure their well-being. You must also confirm that **you will not begin your study until you have received IRB approval**.

- **Benefits of the Study (1 slide)**: Who will benefit from your study? This should be the "wrap-up" slide, giving you a moment to "sell" your study to your committee. (By the way, ONLY your committee members are able to give you their blessings; no one else has the power.)
- **References (1–2 slides)**. Now you will want to add the key references for your presentation. This is one time that you do not have to adhere to a readable font.

How Do You Maintain Composure on the Day of Your Proposal Hearing?

First of all, you **are** the **expert** in the room on your study. You have spent considerable time over the years preparing for this moment. Do not get rattled. You may find that a committee member may introduce another area of study or give a suggestion that makes you feel that it can never be accomplished by you. Keep calm; **know what your research is and what it isn't**. Don't be pulled in a direction that makes it impossible for you to complete.

This is no time to just "wish" that all will go well in your proposal hearing. Roman philosopher Seneca coined the phrase, "Luck is what happens when preparation meets opportunity." **To ensure composure, you need to practice, practice, practice**. You can record your presentation on your phone and listen to it; you can ask your kids to be an audience; or you can find a colleague or another doctoral student to listen to your presentation. The more you rehearse and polish your presentation (cleaning up grammatical errors, making sure it is logical and professional), the greater chance that your committee will give you "the go-ahead."

What Are More Things to Remember on the Day of Your Proposal Hearing?

Words of wisdom for the day of your hearing: Be sure you eat a light meal (and hopefully you are well rested). Bring water. Have handouts of your presentation for your committee and your abstract made available for your audience.

Your nerves may take over, so be prepared. Give yourself plenty of time to allow for problems that could occur, including traffic, parking, rain, snow, earthquake, and so on. Maybe you want to check in with the secretary to confirm the availability of the room and to see if there are any additional forms that need to be completed.

Take time to look at the room at least an hour early in case you need IT's tech help. Check the lighting and the room temperature. If the room is being used when you arrive, don't panic. Find a nice quiet place to enjoy the moment. This too shall pass. You know what you are doing. You are well prepared. Your committee is there to support you.

IT'S SHOWTIME!

Your committee members are all present and ready to begin. Those who are participating remotely are settled and able to hear/see you clearly. Your chair will most probably introduce you. Your title slide is on the screen. You have your notes nearby. Start by introducing your committee, giving thanks first to your chair, and then the others. Now begin. You are becoming an expert on your topic. You will be great!

What Happens After You Finish Your Proposal Hearing Presentation?

Expect your committee to ask questions, as well as others in the room (physically or remotely). Answer the questions to the best of your ability. Ask for clarity if needed. At some point, your chair will ask you (and anyone not on the committee) to leave the room (or sign off if remote) so the committee can deliberate. After a few minutes (which will seem like an eternity), your chair will ask you to return to the room, and will hopefully offer you congratulations: you may begin your study. (*Word of caution:* Your committee can tell you that you need to make minor or major revisions, so be prepared to accept their suggestions.) You have now earned the title: ABD (All but Dissertation) and are now a doctoral candidate.

What Needs to Be Done After Your Proposal Hearing?

You have done a great job! Congratulate yourself. Now it's time to follow up with the details prescribed by your doctoral handbook. You may need to oversee that your chair submits the appropriate signed documents to the department or whatever else is required in your doctoral handbook.

Notes from Your Committee Members. Don't lose the notes you or your chair and committee took during your hearing. You will need to make corrections and include their suggestions in your dissertation.

Institutional Review Board(s) Approval and Other Forms. You, as the Principal (Student) Investigator, are required to submit a signed and completed IRB application. Your chair needs to review it and sign it as the faculty sponsor/supervisor or department chair, whatever your college requires, before you can submit it to the college IRB administrator. Try to pay attention as to when the IRB board convenes, which may impact the turnaround time for your approval. If your approval request comes back needing additional clarification, we suggest that you revise it **immediately** and resubmit it right away.

Now, get going! You are ABD! First, change your future tenses in the first three chapters to align with a completed dissertation (past tense). If you are still waiting for IRB approval, you can start outlining your dissertation's chapter 4 and chapter 5.

13

Dissertation Defense: The Final Frontier

This is your chance to shine—this is original research. Believe it or not, assuming that you did a fabulous job on your proposal hearing (your dress rehearsal), your defense may be less scary. Why, you ask? Because your study is done! The hard work is over. Your proposal hearing could be compared to the preview of a play. Your dissertation defense is like Opening Night. Smile! Now you get to present your findings and enjoy the feedback from your committee.

PREPARING FOR YOUR DISSERTATION DEFENSE

First, breathe. Your nerves will try to get the best of you; don't let them. You have been here before with the proposal hearing as the prelude. Now you are going to focus on what you found from your study and what it means. Make sure that the room/remote link is set, the time is set, the correct forms are filled out, and anything else that needs to be done, according to your doctoral handbook and your chair's suggestions.

Additionally, you must submit copies of your completed dissertation to your chair, and once approved, to the rest of the committee. You will also be required to submit copies of your dissertation to the office/department.

In preparation for the day, you will again create slides to support your talk. Your chair will ask you to submit your presentation slides to the committee ahead of time and have copies of your abstract for those who wish to attend your defense. You have already thoroughly shared

(a) the purpose of your study,
(b) your problem statement,

(c) your research questions,
(d) a synopsis of your literature review, and
(e) the methodology used for your study during your proposal hearing.

Now you can shorten these chapter slides to allow additional time for your findings and results (chapter 4) and your discussion and conclusion (chapter 5), where the bulk of your time should be spent.

The next set of slides are

(f) your findings and analyses of total results, and
(g) your conclusion, including summary of results and emerging themes, implications for practice and legislation, and suggestions for future research.

How Do You Know Which Tables/Figures to Use for Your Defense?

Most probably, your dissertation has many tables and figures. Include only those key tables and figures that highlight your findings. Your tables and figures now become your talking points. This makes it easy for your audience to visually understand the strengths of your research. This also takes the pressure off your need to verbalize each point. All slides, particularly your table and figure slides, should be numbered because when you are finished, your committee will most likely ask questions about a specific slide.

Curtain Up! What Should You Expect During Your Defense?

You have everything set up, including your computer connected to Wi-Fi and to those who are watching remotely, as well as making sure everyone has a seat and is quiet for the seriousness of the moment. Your chair may have assumed these responsibilities—and may have already calmed your nerves by being there ahead of time, allowing you to do a quick rehearsal.

The presentation. Your presentation will most likely follow this format:

- Introduce yourself and welcome everyone.
- Introduce and thank your chair and the rest of your committee.
- Acknowledge any additional faculty, if appropriate.
- Address those who may be participating remotely.
- Now begin. Slow is always best. Read your title and keep going.
- If you stumble or lose your concentration, just go forward.
- Most likely you will have notes in addition to your slides. Try not to read them verbatim. Make it conversational. They are interested in hearing your findings. Use eye contact to engage your audience.

- When you are finished, let them know you are finished with your presentation. Most likely, people will clap. Just say, "Thank you."

Q & A session. Now your chair will take over and lead the questioning session. The purpose of this session is for several reasons:

(a) to clarify what you have found and what you have stated in your presentation,
(b) to make sure that your research has been done by the standards set by the "field,"
(c) to discover what else you may have found in your research that you did not highlight during your presentation, or
(d) to highlight faculty research that may agree (disagree) with your findings.

Responding to your committee's comments and questions. The best way to answer their questions and comments is to first think, "I am *the* expert of my study." Also, be calm and do not become adversarial. Try some of the following hints:

- Repeat the committee member's question before answering it to make sure you heard it correctly (and giving you time to think).
- If a committee member tries to pull you away from the focus of your study, simply state, "I gave quite a bit of thought to what you are asking." Then, restate to the member the quote he/she had said (to confirm that you did hear their point exactly). Finally, calmly say, "I realized that is someone else's study. It was not the focus of my study."
- State your research questions again if you get tongue-tied. That will help keep you focused. This is your moment to shine. Make it your own.

14

You Did It!

You defended your dissertation successfully. Bravo! Now you have additional tasks to complete before receiving that pancake hat. Remember when you first began your doctoral journey and you read the doctoral handbook that you were given? Now it's time to dust it off and read it again, more carefully, because it has key information that you need to complete the doctoral process.

DEADLINES, FORMS, AND UNIVERSITY PROTOCOLS YOU NEED TO FOLLOW

Each university has its own protocols, many of which are spelled out in handbooks or online. However, others may evolve or become known to you during the course of your time there, either sent by mail, by email, or even (sometimes) by word of mouth by professors or other students. Take note; write them into your calendar and be ready to comply with them when the time comes.

Deadlines. Speaking of calendars, from the very beginning, as we have talked about before, you will want to keep your calendar up to date. Each time you meet with your chair, jot it into your calendar (and keep your notes from the meeting in a dissertation info folder). This will help in the future in case anything is missing.

Also, add your timeline into your calendar on future dates that you may anticipate having each section completed. Insert when to have in all paperwork—from taking the comps to applying for graduation. This way you will be better prepared to successfully complete each step in a timely manner.

Forms and Graduation. Believe it or not, many students miss out on their graduation because they **did not complete the graduation form** before the close-out date. At this point, you should be a "bureaucrat." Keep all paperwork completed on time, noting dates, the person who received it, copies of it, and so on, in a folder. Years later, you will appreciate learning this discipline and use it for completing other tasks as well.

PUBLISHING IN PROQUEST

So, now you have completed your dissertation and want to get it published. Most dissertations are published in ProQuest. Make sure to check with your university to see where they require you to publish.

Here is the address, phone number, and website for ProQuest to get you started:

Address: ProQuest LLC.
789 East Eisenhower Parkway
P.O. Box 1346
Ann Arbor, MI 48106
Telephone: 800–521–0600
Website: http://www.proquest.com/enUS/products/dissertations/individuals.shtml

WRITE AN ARTICLE BASED ON YOUR DISSERTATION FINDINGS

You, and perhaps your chair as a co-author, will want to write an article for an academic peer-reviewed journal to summarize highlights of what your study found.

You can send your dissertation (summary) to a scholarly association that recognizes outstanding dissertations. They may send you a monetary award or support your conference fees for you to present at their next conference. Check with educational conferences, such as the American Association of School Administrators (AASA), American Educational Research Association (AERA), Association for Supervision and Curriculum Development (ASCD), National Association of Elementary School Principals (NAESP), and National Association of Secondary School Principals (NASSP) and their state affiliates.

THANK ALL WHO HELPED YOU THROUGH THIS PROCESS

Ah, this is the most fun part of the journey! Between the two of us, we have received thank-you cards, Starbucks coffee cards and other gift cards, appreciation phone calls, flowers, and more. We truly feel blessed just to know when one of our students has completed their doctoral journey. The greatest reward for all of us is to say, "Congratulations, Doctor. Welcome to the Club!"

Yes, it also is the time to thank your family (maybe even reintroduce yourself because they may have forgotten your name!), your friends, and those shopkeepers that personally saw you through by getting your coffee early in the morning or late at night, and the like. Many people will be thrilled to hear you say, "I've finished! I'm a doctor now!"

You may have also asked professionals along the way, such as other researchers, state and federal agency employees, librarians, and authors of books that you read six times over, for their assistance. This is a terrific time to send them an email and thank them for their help and guidance.

CHANGE YOUR VITA!

Your vita now has new meaning. So you will want to update the "Education" section (which for Ed.D. folks is usually the first category on the vita). You will also want to add your dissertation to the books and publication section, as you have now written your first book. Once you have your ProQuest number and website address, you can add that too.

If you are not already teaching at the college level, it is a wonderful time to apply for a full-time or adjunct position at a college or university. It is also a time that you can join the ranks of an association and assume greater responsibilities in leadership.

Take a leap and apply for that job you have always wanted. You may not get hired on the first few attempts, as the pool is now filled with others with your credentials. However, on the positive side, the pool is MUCH shallower, as fewer people will have the needed qualifications. Don't wait to become (a) older (or younger, which by the way, never happens!), (b) more experienced (doesn't matter now—you have proved that you can do anything!), or (c) anything else you want to use as an excuse. DO IT NOW!

GO TO GRADUATION (YOUR LAST ONE!)

This is one graduation **you do not want to miss**. Jan still remembers going to her doctoral graduation at Columbia and hearing Harry Belafonte singing, "Banana Boat Song (Day-O)" with all 30,000 people on the university lawn joining in. Paula remembers wearing her pancake hat as shade while by the Arch in Washington Square for her NYU doctoral graduation.

Figure 14.1. Wearing of the Pancake Hat! (Dissertation Chair Jan Hammond with newly graduated Drs. Kimberly Strothers, Paula Beck, and Janet Kiley). ***Jan Hammond, photographer.***

So, don't lose this moment to invite those very close to you (usually limited tickets). At the end of the ceremony, take hundreds of pictures with colleagues, faculty, and family. And feel free to put that pancake hat on someone who has been with you throughout the whole struggle—or whole lifetime—like your parents, spouse, or even children. This truly is your moment to relish the joy of completing a lifetime goal.

Epilogue

Your Continued Contribution to the Field

Ahem, you are **not** stopping here. As you are now a "Member of the Club," you need to continue to write, research, take leadership positions, present at national conferences, and contribute to the field of education. This is your turn now to give back and help others in their quest to improve the educational system for children and adults at all levels.

You will find that you are now being asked to (a) participate in accreditation associations (e.g., Middle States Association or Council for the Accreditation of Educator Preparation), (b) become a board member of educational associations, or (c) serve on committees for state/federal agencies and departments. This is your time to share your writing and research skills with those who need your expertise and higher-level thinking skills.

You may also be asked to be a member of a doctoral dissertation committee. Despite the heavy reading and support that you will be giving to your doctoral student, you will gain much enjoyment, just as we have, in seeing the struggles and accomplishments of your student. Perhaps you, too, may be ready to now write your next book.

FINAL WORDS OF WISDOM
Don't keep asking everybody about the best topic for your dissertation. You will drive yourself nuts. Just choose a topic and stick to it. *Do* keep a *Then and There* habit. When you open mail, answer it at that moment. Put things away as soon as you use them. Put keys and phone in the same place **always**. *Do* keep your focus on the long-term goal. *Don't* lose your integrity. Don't plagiarize. Don't take shortcuts. *Do* prioritize. Family first. Be there for "firsts" and important family days, because they won't happen again. Remember another quote: *Lost time is never found again* (Ben Franklin). *Don't* have your dissertation scattered in many different areas of the house or office. *Do* take time off (a few days) from school or work once you receive your data and are nearing the end. Lock yourself in a hotel room if necessary to write your Chapter IV and/or Chapter V (your last two chapters). *Don't* force it. Sleep on it. Maybe get up at 4:30 a.m. when you are feeling fresh. *Do* your best job always, including your assignments and participating in classes. *Don't* get frustrated. Don't give up. Keep your eyes on the prize. *Do* keep in balance. Find healthy snacks; get eight hours of rest, and exercise. *Don't* give up everything in your life. Life is going on. *Do* keep spiritual. Schedule time for yourself to pray, meditate, and show love. *Do* know when *enough is enough* for the day. Stop writing and go to bed. *Do* set realistic goals. Know your limits.
Do keep lists. You cannot memorize everything. It's a nice feeling when you can cross things off your list. *Don't* keep going. Know when the literature review is done. Learn to stop. *Do* take breaks. Take a walk with friends. Have a coffee. Call a friend to regain energy. *Do* be grateful. You are doing God's Work. No one else can do what you are doing.

Figure E.1. Final Words of Wisdom. ***Jan Hammond and Paula Lester.***

Appendix

Exempt Status for IRB Approval

EXEMPT

(1) Research, conducted in established or commonly accepted educational settings, that specifically involves normal educational practices that are not likely to adversely impact students' opportunity to learn required educational content or the assessment of educators who provide instruction. This includes most research on regular and special education instructional strategies, and research on the effectiveness of or the comparison among instructional techniques, curricula, or classroom management methods.

(2) Research that only includes interactions involving educational tests (cognitive, diagnostic, aptitude, achievement), survey procedures, interview procedures, or observation of public behavior (including visual or auditory recording) if at least one of the following criteria is met: (i) The information obtained is recorded by the investigator in such a manner that the identity of the human subjects cannot readily be ascertained, directly or through identifiers linked to the subjects; (ii) Any disclosure of the human subjects' responses outside the research would not reasonably place the subjects at risk of criminal or civil liability or be damaging to the subjects' financial standing, employability, educational advancement, or reputation; or (iii) The information obtained is recorded by the investigator in such a manner that the identity of the human subjects can readily be ascertained, directly or through identifiers linked to the subjects, and an IRB conducts a limited IRB review to make the determination required by §46.111(a)(7).

(3) (i) Research involving benign behavioral interventions in conjunction with the collection of information from an adult subject through verbal or written responses (including data entry) or audiovisual recording if the subject prospectively agrees to the intervention and information collection and

at least one of the following criteria is met: (A) The information obtained is recorded by the investigator in such a manner that the identity of the human subjects cannot readily be ascertained, directly or through identifiers linked to the subjects; (B) Any disclosure of the human subjects' responses outside the research would not reasonably place the subjects at risk of criminal or civil liability or be damaging to the subjects' financial standing, employability, educational advancement, or reputation; or (C) The information obtained is recorded by the investigator in such a manner that the identity of the human subjects can readily be ascertained, directly or through identifiers linked to the subjects, and an IRB conducts a limited IRB review to make the determination required by §46.111(a)(7). (ii) For the purpose of this provision, benign behavioral interventions are brief in duration, harmless, painless, not physically invasive, not likely to have a significant adverse lasting impact on the subjects, and the investigator has no reason to think the subjects will find the interventions offensive or embarrassing. Provided all such criteria are met, examples of such benign behavioral interventions would include having the subjects play an online game, having them solve puzzles under various noise conditions, or having them decide how to allocate a nominal amount of received cash between themselves and someone else. (iii) If the research involves deceiving the subjects regarding the nature or purposes of the research, this exemption is not applicable unless the subject authorizes the deception through a prospective agreement to participate in research in circumstances in which the subject is informed that he or she will be unaware of or misled regarding the nature or purposes of the research.

(4) Secondary research for which consent is not required: Secondary research uses of identifiable private information or identifiable biospecimens, if at least one of the following criteria is met: (i) The identifiable private information or identifiable biospecimens are publicly available; (ii) Information, which may include information about biospecimens, is recorded by the investigator in such a manner that the identity of the human subjects cannot readily be ascertained directly or through identifiers linked to the subjects, the investigator does not contact the subjects, and the investigator will not re-identify subjects; (iii) The research involves only information collection and analysis involving the investigator's use of identifiable health information when that use is regulated under 45 CFR parts 160 and 164, subparts A and E, for the purposes of "health care operations" or "research" as those terms are defined at 45 CFR 164.501 or for "public health activities and purposes" as described under 45 CFR 164.512(b); or (iv) The research is conducted by, or on behalf of, a Federal department or agency using government-generated or government-collected information obtained for non-research activities, if the research generates identifiable private information that is or will be main-

tained on information technology that is subject to and in compliance with section 208(b) of the E-Government Act of 2002, 44 U.S.C. 3501. Note, if all of the identifiable private information collected, used, or generated as part of the activity will be maintained in systems of records subject to the Privacy Act of 1974, 5 U.S.C. 552a, and, if applicable, the information used in the research was collected subject to the Paperwork Reduction Act of 1995, 44 U.S.C. 3501 et seq.

(5) Research and demonstration projects that are conducted or supported by a Federal department or agency, or otherwise subject to the approval of department or agency heads (or the approval of the heads of bureaus or other subordinate agencies that have been delegated authority to conduct the research and demonstration projects), and that are designed to study, evaluate, improve, or otherwise examine public benefit or service programs, including procedures for obtaining benefits or services under those programs, possible changes in or alternatives to those programs or procedures, or possible changes in methods or levels of payment for benefits or services under those programs. Such projects include, but are not limited to, internal studies by Federal employees, and studies under contracts or consulting arrangements, cooperative agreements, or grants. Exempt projects also include waivers of otherwise mandatory requirements using authorities such as sections 1115 and 1115A of the Social Security Act, as amended.

(6) Taste and food quality evaluation and consumer acceptance studies: (i) If wholesome foods without additives are consumed, or (ii) If a food is consumed that contains a food ingredient at or below the level and for a use found to be safe, or agricultural chemical or environmental contaminant at or below the level found to be safe, by the Food and Drug Administration or approved by the Environmental Protection Agency or the Food Safety and Inspection Service of the U.S. Department of Agriculture.

(7) Storage or maintenance for secondary research for which broad consent is required: Storage or maintenance of identifiable private information or identifiable biospecimens for potential secondary research use if an IRB conducts a limited IRB review and makes the determinations required by §46.111(a)(8).

(8) Secondary research for which broad consent is required: Research involving the use of identifiable private information or identifiable biospecimens for secondary research use, if the following criteria are met: (i) Broad consent for the storage, maintenance, and secondary research use of the identifiable private information or identifiable biospecimens was obtained in accordance with §46.116(a)(1) through (4), (a)(6), and (d); (ii) Documentation of informed consent or waiver of documentation of consent was obtained in accordance with §46.117; (iii) An IRB conducts a limited IRB review and

makes the determination required by §46.111(a)(7) and makes the determination that the research to be conducted is within the scope of the broad consent referenced in paragraph (d)(8)(i) of this section; and (iv) The investigator does not include returning individual research results to subjects as part of the study plan. This provision does not prevent an investigator from abiding by any legal requirements to return individual research results.

References

Anderson, N., Schlueter, J. E., Carlson, J. F., & Geisinger, K. F. (Eds.). (2016). *Tests in print IX*. Buros Center for Testing.

Beck, P. D. (2014). *Fourth-grade students' subjective interactions with the seven elements of art: An exploratory case study using Q-methodology*. (Publication No. 3666682) (Doctoral dissertation, Long Island University, C. W. Post Center). ProQuest Dissertations and Theses Global. Web. 11 Jan. 2021.

Berger, D. A. (2014) *"I do as much as any teacher"—Role conflict among paraeducators in private special education schools*. (Publication No. 3672820) (Doctoral dissertation, Long Island University, C. W. Post Center). ProQuest Dissertations and Theses Global. Web. 11 Jan. 2021.

Berkowicz, J., & Myers, A. (2018, May 15). Leadership endings and personal lessons. *EdWeek*. http://blogs.edweek.org/edweek/leadership_360/.

Buros Mental Measurements (2020). *The twenty-first mental measurement yearbook* (21st ed.). Edited by Janet F. Carlson, Kurt F. Geisinger, and Jessica L. Jonson. Hardbound, LC 39-3422, ISBN 978-0-910674-68-3.

Chagares, A. M. (2016). *Experienced teachers' stated preferences regarding transferring from well-performing to low-performing schools: A discrete choice experiment*. (Publication No. 10135066) (Doctoral dissertation, Long Island University, C. W. Post Center). ProQuest Dissertations and Theses Global. Web. 11 Jan. 2021.

Cohen, L., Manion, L., & Morrison, K. (2017). *Research methods for education* (8th ed.). Routledge.

Collaborative Institutional Training Initiative (CITI Program) (n.d.). *The trusted standard in research, ethics, and compliance training* (www.citiprogram.org). Retrieved January 28, 2021, from https://about.citiprogram.org/en/homepage/.

Corey, C. M. (2015). *A study of instructional scheduling, teaming, and common planning in New York State Middle Schools*. (Publication No. 3682855) (Doctoral dissertation, Seton Hall University). ProQuest Dissertations and Theses Global. Web. 23 Jan. 2021.

Creswell, J. (2013). *Qualitative inquiry & research design*, 3rd ed. Sage Publications, Inc.

Dubin, R. (1978). *Theory building* (2nd ed.). Free Press.

Fliegner, Herbert R. (1984). *School leadership and organizational health: A simulated teaching unit.* Dissertation Abstracts International.

Jaccard, J., & Jacoby, J. (2020). *Theory construction and model building skills* (2nd ed.). Guilford Press.

Kellner, M. F. (2019). *Admissions criteria that best predict which applicants will successfully enter the nursing profession.* (Publication No. 13425823) (Doctoral dissertation, Long Island University, C. W. Post Center). ProQuest Dissertations and Theses Global. Web. 11 Jan. 2021.

Kuhn, T. S. (2012). *The structure of scientific revolutions.* University of Chicago Press.

Lester, P., Inman, D., & Bishop, L. (2014). *Handbook of tests and measurement in education and the social sciences* (3rd ed.). Rowman & Littlefield Publications.

Maslow, A. (1943). A theory of human motivation. *Psychological Review*, 50, 370–96. http://psychclassics.yorku.ca/Maslow/motivation.htm.

McGregor, D. (1960). *The human side of enterprise.* McGraw-Hill Publishers.

Miles, M. B., & Huberman, A. M. (1994). *Qualitative data analysis: An expanded sourcebook.* Thousand Oaks.

New York State School Boards Association (2020). *School law* (38th ed.). Acknowledgment. LexisNexis, p. xix.

Norris, T., Vines, P. L., & Hoeffel, E. M. (2012). *The American Indian and Alaska Native population: 2010.* U.S. Department of Commerce, Economics, and Statistics Administration, U.S. Census Bureau.

Nunnally, J. C. (1978). *Psychometric theory* (2nd ed.). McGraw-Hill.

Popper, K. (1959). *The logic of scientific discovery.* Basic Books.

Publication Manual of the American Psychological Association (2019, August). *7th edition APA's best-selling "Publication Manual" to publish in October with 700,000 first printing.* https://www.apa.org>press>2019/08

Rounds, L. (1954). *A plan for meeting the post-high school educational needs of older youth in Rockland County.* Dissertation, Columbia University.

Sax, G. (1968). *Empirical foundations of educational research.* Prentice-Hall.

Strunk Jr., W. & White, E. B. (2018). *The Elements of Style.* Thriftbooks.

SUNY Rockland Community College (n.d.). *Transforming vision to reality (1954–1959).* Retrieved January 28, 2021, from https://rcc60th.com/history-of-rcc/.

Swanson, R. A., & Chermack, T. J. (2013). *Theory building in applied disciplines.* Berrett-Koehler Publishers, Inc.

Swanson, R. A., & Holton, E. F. (2009). *Research in organizations: Foundations and methods in inquiry.* Berrett-Koehler Publishers, Inc.

Velastegui, P. J. (2013). *Naturally-emerging technology-based leadership roles in three independent schools: A social network-based case study using fuzzy set qualitative comparative analysis.* (Publication No. 3608798) (Doctoral dissertation, Long Island University, C. W. Post Center). ProQuest Dissertations and Theses Global. Web. 12 Jan. 2021.

Zahedi, K. J. (2010). *Middle school teacher satisfaction with response to intervention (RtI): An assessment between inception and implementation*. (Publication No. 3402684) (State University of New York at Albany). ProQuest Dissertations and Theses Global. Web. 23 Jan. 2021.

Zinsser, William (2013). *On writing well: The classic guide to writing nonfiction* (30th year ed.). Allyn & Bacon, a Pearson Education Company.

Index

About the Authors

Dr. Jan P. Hammond is professor emerita at the State University of New York at New Paltz where she was department chair and director of the doctoral program between SUNY and the University at Albany and has served on numerous dissertation committees. With nearly 50 years in education, she has held leadership positions at the K–12 level as well as on state and national boards and associations. She has received numerous awards including the SUNY Excellence in Teaching award and New York State Educator of the Year. She has written extensively on educational leadership, competitive advantage for schools, and mentoring. Dr. Hammond received her Ed.D. from Columbia University, where, in 1993, she was honored at the Teachers College Alumni Day for her outstanding dissertation titled "School Choice and Student Performance."

Dr. Paula E. Lester brings to this resource 50 years of experience as a university professor and department chairperson, dissertation chairperson, dissertation committee member, educational administrator, and classroom teacher. She received a Ph.D. in organizational and administrative studies from New York University and she was awarded the Outstanding Dissertation of the Year award from the Association of Supervision and Curriculum Development. Her more than 25 publications include six books and articles in *Educational and Psychological Measurement*, *Principal*, *Clearing House*, and other periodicals. She has been on the faculty of Long Island University since 1985 and is currently a senior professor. She received the Newton Award for Academic Excellence as well as numerous research grants from the university. In addition, Dr. Lester is the founding director of the doctoral program in interdisciplinary educational studies at Long Island University.

Printed in the USA
CPSIA information can be obtained
at www.ICGtesting.com
LVHW092007091123
763520LV00002B/11

9 781475 850109